MW01050675

Zondervan/Youth Specialties Books

OPTION PLAYS

60 CREATIVE DILEMMAS TO HELP YOUR KIDS LEARN EFFECTIVE DECISION MAKING

CHAP CLARK, DUFFY ROBBINS, MIKE YACONELLI
EDITED BY NOEL BECCHETTI

Youth Specialties

ZONDERVAN PUBLISHING HOUSE
Grand Rapids, Michigan

Option Plays

Copyright © 1990 by Youth Specialties, Inc.

Youth Specialties Books, 1224 Greenfield Drive, El Cajon, California 92021, are published by
Zondervan Publishing House, 1415 Lake Drive, S.E., Grand Rapids, Michigan 49506

Library of Congress Cataloging-in-Publication Data

Clark, Chap, 1954-
    Option plays : 60 creative dilemmas to help your kids learn effective decision making / Chap
Clark, Duffy Robbins, Mike Yaconelli : edited by Noel Becchetti.

    p.   cm.
    ISBN 0-310-53401-1
    1. Decision-making—Religious aspects—Christianity. 2. Youth—Religious life. 3. Decision-
making in adolescence. I. Robbins, Duffy. II. Yaconelli, Mike. III. Becchetti, Noel. 1955- . IV.
Title.
    BV4531.2.C515   1990
    268'.433—dc20   90-38500
                                           CIP

All Scripture quotations, unless otherwise noted, are taken from the *Holy Bible: New International
Version* (North American Edition). Copyright © 1973, 1978, 1984 by the International Bible Society.
Used by permission of Zondervan Bible Publishers.

The material in this book may be photocopied for local use in churches, youth groups, and other
Christian-education activities. Special permission is not necessary. However, the contents of this
book may not be reproduced in any other form without written permission from the publisher. All
rights reserved.

Edited by Noel Becchetti
Designed by Dan Pegoda
Typography by Leah Perry

Printed in the United States of America

90 91 92 93 94 95 96 97 98 99 / **AK** / 10 9 8 7 6 5 4 3 2 1

About the *YOUTHSOURCE*™ Publishing Group

YOUTHSOURCE™ books, tapes, videos, and other resources pool the expertise of three of the finest youth-ministry resource providers in the world:

Campus Life Books—publishers of the award-winning *Campus Life* magazine, who for nearly fifty years have helped high schoolers live Christian lives.

Youth Specialties—serving ministers to middle-school, junior-high, and high-school youth for over twenty years through books, magazines, and training events such as the National Youth Workers Convention.

Zondervan Publishing House—one of the oldest, largest, and most respected evangelical Christian publishers in the world.

Campus Life
465 Gundersen Dr.
Carol Stream, IL 60188
708/260-6200

Youth Specialties
1224 Greenfield Dr.
El Cajon, CA 92021
619/440-2333

Zondervan
1415 Lake Dr. S.E.
Grand Rapids, MI 49506
616/698-6900

CONTENTS

PREFACE

One of the great challenges in youth ministry is helping our kids learn to make wise decisions. In our combined youth-ministry experience, we've found that keeping kids from either blindly following the lead of their peers or unthinkingly internalizing the pearls of "wisdom" that we've taught is an ongoing and critical task. It's in our ability to help our young people along the road to mature decision making, stemming from a live Christian faith and grounded in biblical values, that we fulfill our calling as youth ministers.

But helping kids to learn decision-making skills isn't easy. How do we keep our youth from stampeding toward "pat" answers that, although ultimately self-defeating, create a sense of quick resolution? How do we help them grapple with the truths of Scripture when they seemingly collide with difficult real-life issues?

It was in the hope of providing all of us with a tool to teach decision-making skills that *Option Plays* was developed. We've found that giving kids real-life scenarios that, although fictional, replicate experiences that they have gone through or will likely face in the near future, helps them to discover, access, and integrate Christian truth at a level not achievable by other means. The overwhelming acceptance of Youth Specialties' *Tension Getters* series, *TalkSheet*™ discussion starters, and interactive curricula, such as *Up Close and Personal: How to Build Community in Your Youth Group* and *Teaching the Truth about Sex*, are all cases in point. And the fun of wrestling through these tension-creating scenarios adds incredible spark and zest to the learning process—something no youth worker can do without!

We offer these *Option Plays* with the sincere hope that you'll find them to be an invaluable addition to your youth-ministry "tool kit" as you seek to bring God's love and the hope of Christ to the young people under your care. Thank you for your interest in, and care for, kids. Yours is one of the highest callings.

TOPICAL INDEX

Each Option Play focuses on one or more of the following issues. Under each topic below, the Option Plays that apply are listed by number. *These are not page numbers.* They are the numbers (1-60) assigned to each of the 60 Option Plays. They appear at the top of the page with each Option Play.

Abortion, 10

AIDS, 28

Alcohol, 7, 11, 20, 21, 37

Cheating, 11, 58, 60

Chemical dependency, 7, 20, 21, 29

Church, 7, 16, 25, 32, 35, 40, 47, 50, 55

Crime, 29, 33, 38, 45

Dating, 1, 4, 5, 10, 30, 36, 39, 41, 43, 55

Dealing with authority, 9, 11, 12, 13, 15, 16, 22, 24, 32, 45, 50, 52, 54, 56, 59

Death and dying, 28

Disability, 43

Discipleship, 8, 37, 50, 53, 57

Divorce, 1, 3, 13, 18

Drinking, 7, 11, 20, 21, 37

Drinking and driving, 21

Drugs, 2, 29, 31, 45, 46

Ethics, 1, 10, 11, 15, 22, 31, 33, 34, 38, 42, 45, 48, 53, 54, 55, 56, 60

Evangelism, 8, 37, 45, 46, 49, 50, 53, 55, 59, 60

Family relationships, 1, 2, 9, 12, 13, 15, 16, 17, 18, 19, 20, 32, 50, 52, 54, 59

Fighting, 42, 51

Forced (blended) families, 1, 13, 18

Forgiveness, 2, 13, 14, 21, 33, 58

Friendship, 6, 7, 14, 22, 23, 26, 27, 29, 30, 31, 33, 34, 36, 38, 39, 41, 42, 43, 45, 46, 47, 48, 53, 57, 58, 59, 60

Gambling, 33

Gangs, 42

Homosexuality, 6, 14

Honesty, 1, 3, 5, 6, 7, 9, 10, 14, 17, 21, 25, 34, 38, 43, 44, 45, 46, 54, 58, 60

Interracial relations, 30, 55

Judging others, 8, 57, 58, 59

Legal issues and responsibilities, 26, 37, 38, 41, 45

Section One

PRE-GAME WARMUPS

Chapter **ONE**

*U*NDERSTANDING AND USING OPTION MAKING AND CONSEQUENCING

Mike Yaconelli

*N*o one likes to make decisions. We would rather have someone else make the decisions for us. Why? We're lazy. The truth is that the process of decision making is work. *Option Plays* is an exercise in decision making. It asks adolescents to do what they don't want to do—make decisions. But they are being asked to do more than make decisions; they are being asked to make wise, informed, thoughtful decisions.

Decisions made in the trenches of life require two basic thinking skills: *option making* and *consequencing*.

Option Making

Option making is the ability to construct all of the options created by a particular *decision moment*. A decision moment occurs when a life situation requires a choice to be made. Options are alternatives created by a given situation. Option making is the skill that allows the decision maker to understand and define all of the possible decisions that could be made in any situation. It is the ability to answer the question: "What *can* I do?"

Let's say, for example, that you are a high school student who is at a party where many of the kids are drinking. You are being encouraged to drink by a group of friends who make it clear to you that if you don't drink, they will consider you an outsider. Option making is the ability to look at the situation and create as many alternatives as possible:

1. You could not drink any alcohol.
2. You could have one drink.
3. You could drink as much as you want.
4. You could pretend to drink alcohol but consume a soft drink instead.
5. You could think of a clever reason why you can't drink.
6. You could leave the party.

The better you are at creating alternatives, the more able you are to cope with a situation.

Consequencing

Consequencing is the ability to project the results of our decisions. It is the ability to answer the question: "If I choose this option, what will happen?" It is possibility thinking in that it generates all the possibile results of a decision. Using the example above, let's suppose a person chooses option #2 (You could have one drink). Consequencing is thinking through all the possible consequences if you were to make that decision:

1. Your friends will think you are cool.
2. Now that you have had one drink, the pressure to drink more will increase.
3. You could disappoint a lot of your friends who respected you for not drinking.
4. Your parents might detect the alcohol, which could result in losing driving privileges, going on restriction, and eroding the trust between yourself and your parents.
5. You might decide to drink more.
6. Your friends, who encouraged you to drink, might turn on you and ridicule you calling you a hypocrite.

Consequencing prepares you for the effects of your decision making. It keeps you from being surprised by what happens and it allows you to see the effects of a decision without actually having to live through them.

Option Plays is an exercise book. It takes work, mental work, to go through each of the exercises, but we think the results are worth the effort.

Answers to the Most Frequently Asked Questions About Option Making and Consequencing

Shouldn't we make sure kids choose the right option rather than simply teaching them how to understand and create options?

We should emphasize *both*. The trouble in the church is that we have emphasized the right answer for so long that it has never occurred to us that in order for an answer to be "right" there must be at least one or more answers that are "wrong." I put "right" and "wrong" in quotes deliberately because when it comes to almost all of our decisions, "right" means the best decision under the circumstances and "wrong" means a less-than-best decision under those same circumstances. Of course, there are decisions where right and wrong are clear, moral, and biblical. But most decisions are, unfortunately, not that easy. We must choose between options that are the most right or the least wrong. Our choice may be based on biblical principles, but those principles may not deal specifically with the particular dilemma we are facing at that moment.

We in the church have also taught, either overtly or by implication, that God always gives us but one narrow path, incorporating one specific plan, to follow. Consequently, decision making is perceived as a treasure hunt rather than a fox hunt. In a treasure hunt, the treasure is hidden and we must find its exact location. In a fox hunt, we are chasing the fox. We know what the fox looks like, but we have no idea where it is going. We have to follow as closely as we can and try to predict what the fox will do next.

Decision making is not finding the hidden treasure of the one "right" answer; rather it is a chase, a complicated search for the elusive fox of truth. *Making the "right" decision is a skill that can only be learned in the battleground of possible decisions.*

Why don't we just tell kids what to decide?

Telling adolescents *what* to do doesn't help them to understand *why* they are doing it. And ultimately, our ministry is not to tell them what to do in a particular situation; our ministry is to equip them to know how to make wise decisions when they're on their own.

Adolescents are too easily influenced by adults they admire and respect. Telling them what to do will influence them for the moment, but teaching them how to decide what to do will influence them for the rest of their lives.

What part do absolutes play in decision making?

To suggest that most decisions are determined by the situation does not mean that one believes in situation ethics or relative truth. Absolute truth has relative consequences, and it can be applied in a variety of ways depending on the circumstances.

The absolute truth is very important. But once kids understand the absolute truth, they must then decide how that absolute truth applies in specific situations.

What is more important—absolute truth or the ability to make a decision?

Both. If absolute truth is emphasized at the expense of the ability to make a decision, we have totalitarianism. If the ability to make a decision is emphasized at the expense of absolute truth, we have relativism. There is a healthy tension between the two that must be juggled if we are to ensure a healthy decision-making process.

It Is *How You Play the Game*

We admit that in the case of the exercises found in *Option Plays*, we consider teaching adolescents the ability to make decisions to be more important than articulating a particular absolute truth. We are more concerned with helping kids learn how to fish than helping them catch the fish. It is difficult for us to keep from making decisions for our kids, because we care about them and don't want to see them suffer the consequences of bad decisions. But we are convinced that the more we can help students make their own decisions, the more able they'll be to make "right" decisions, based on their Christian faith, in the real worlds that they live in.

Chapter **TWO**

*H*ELPING TEENAGERS MAKE WISE DECISIONS

Duffy Robbins

My favorite brain teaser begins with a father who goes out to buy a pet for his children. Like most dads, he wants his kids to be happy. He would do almost anything to see a big grin on the faces of his two little girls.

He hadn't actually planned to that Saturday morning, but he ended up at a farm out in the country. And before he knew it, he had bought his family a horse for the bargain price of six dollars! He couldn't believe his good fortune. He was ecstatic. The kids were going to love it.

And love it they did. When he rode that horse into the living room just before lunch that Saturday morning, it was as if he were an emperor returning from battle. The kids were cheering, the dog was barking, and his wife was smiling—well, sort of.

By the following Wednesday, the dog had calmed down, the kids were still in love with "Calico," and his wife had threatened to leave. The horse was not house-trained, and the vacuum cleaner simply was not suited to the kinds of tasks that were being asked of it. The wife gave the ultimatum: It's me or the horse, but one of us is going to gallop.

Dad knew she was right. There was no way they could keep an animal like that around the house. So he reluctantly took the horse back to the farmer who had originally sold it to him and sold it back for eight dollars.

It was a sad scene at dinner that night. Everybody missed Calico. And it seemed that Dad missed the horse more than the kids. After the kids had gone to bed, Dad went out on the back porch and stared at the night sky with a sad look on his face, then sang old cowboy songs.

After about a week of this, the wife announced that she had changed her mind. She couldn't stand to see everybody moping around the house. "Go back and get the horse, if that's what you really want to do," she sighed.

Dad and the kids were in the car within minutes. Maybe they could get old Calico back. Calico was still there. She hadn't been sold yet. But the price had skyrocketed to ten dollars! It was an outrage, "But this is Calico," Dad said. "We'll take it!"

There was joy in the house that day, and cowboy hoots, and laughter. Just like old times. But, just like old times, Calico was having a cleanliness problem, and the bad situations just kept piling up. Finally, the hand-writing was on the stall. Calico had to go.

It was decided that they'd try to return Calico to the same farmer so that she could be out at her old corral again. And the farmer did buy her back—for twelve dollars.

After all was said and done, one question remained: Did Dad make or lose money on the deal? And if so, how much either way? Before you read any further in this chapter, try to come up with an answer. Don't try to factor in the cost of hay or gas to and from the farm. Just base your answer on the straight math.

A Little Horse Trading

You have likely come up with one of the following answers: Dad (a) lost four dollars; (b) lost two dollars; (c) broke even; (d) made two dollars; (e) made four dollars; (f) made six dollars; (g) I don't care—let's get on with the book!

For those of you who do care, when all of the horse trading was over and the dust had settled, old Dad broke even. If that's the answer you came up with, stop right now and give yourself a hand.

Now, if you've been giving yourself a hand, stop—because the answer given in the above paragraph is wrong. I just wanted to see if I could trick you. The real answer is . . . Dad lost two dollars. Go back and figure it out again and you will see how easy it is.

If you went back and refigured, you know that I lied again. The answer given in the paragraph above is also untrue. That was just some more horse-trading fun. The real answer is that Dad made four dollars.

At this point you are skipping down the page to see if this really is the right answer. It is. And some of you by now would not believe any answer that I gave for this problem, because you've already been lied to twice. You're not really sure what the answer is.

Welcome to Reality

If you've emerged from that word problem slightly befuddled, you can begin to understand what it's like to be a teenager trying to make wise decisions. In the first place, the answers aren't always so obvious. Even when people say "It's easy" or "Just Say No," one quickly discovers that it's not all that simple. Trusted people give us bad advice. Some give us incorrect answers. Others lie to us. We aren't completely confident whom to listen to and whom we can trust.

And bear in mind that the little horse-trading exercise we've just finished is from a second-grade math book. How much more complex is decision making when the issues are literally life-shaping? That's what it's like trying to make wise decisions as a teenager.

In the real world, bad decisions don't usually come wrapped in second-grade math problems, and the price for believing the wrong answer is usually more than a slap at the forehead and a smile of embarrassment. In his book, *Going to Extremes* (Plume/Penguin Books), author Joe McGinnis gives us a graphic picture of the tuition one pays for lessons learned the hard way in real life:

> Yesterday's evidence of the predatory nature and the overwhelming power of the grizzly had made a strong impression, and this skin of verbal protection within which we were trying to encase ourselves (the guide had commented that '99.9 percent of the time a grizzly bear would not attack a hiker') seemed pretty thin. Especially with the memory of the bear in the night still so vivid. Even if he had, eventually, run away. That had not been a paw print; that had not been just a blond hair in a tree; that had not been simply evidence of a kill from months before. That had been a live grizzly bear. Weighing four hundred pounds, maybe five hundred pounds. Standing only fifty yards from us and staring at us. It was going to take more than probability theory to make me feel comfortable.
>
> Well, Ray (the guide) said, upon further consideration, a grizzly would be reluctant to charge a group of hikers. One person, or two, might be different. The trouble was, no one really knew for sure. The evidence, such as it was, was based only on input from survivors. People like ourselves, who had witnessed a bear behaving in a non-aggressive manner. The people toward whom a bear behaved aggressively generally did not get to deliver their reports.

One of the reasons we must take the time to help students make wise decisions is because the cost for bad decisions is just too high. It isn't easy, and it won't be quick. But helping students to make wise decisions may be one of the most important life skills that we can teach them as they move through adolescence.

Why Do Teenagers Make Bad Decisions?

There are probably as many reasons for teenagers making bad decisions as there are teenagers. If we are going to help teenagers make wise decisions, we need to take into account some of the reasons for their unwise decisions.

Overbearing parents

Earl Wilson, in his book *You Try Being A Teenager* (Multnomah Press), notes that parents actually hinder their children's opportunities to learn decision-making skills by making one of three mistakes: underestimating the problem ("It's obvious what you should do"), overestimating the problem ("You're thinking about what?!"), or taking decision-making responsibility away from their children ("I'll decide what's best for you"). How will kids learn to make wise decisions if they're not allowed to learn decision making?

Lack of convictions

Somewhere along the line, we forgot that if we want students to "Just Say No" to something, we've got to encourage them first to "Just Say Yes" to something else. Most teenagers today simply have no convictions. They have grown up in a culture that refuses to admit to any set standards of right and wrong. As John Naisbitt wrote in his book, *Megatrends*, we live no longer in an "either-or generation"; it is now a "multiple-choice generation."

When faced with decisions and armed with no real sense of right and wrong, it is tough to know which is the right decision to make.

Naive peers

Teenagers make bad decisions because they rely on the judgment of friends who are making equally bad decisions. Adolescents do not really understand just how naive they are. They may be "sophisticated"; they may have experienced a lot in a short time. But they have not experienced time, and time is often the greatest teacher. The more time that passes, the more history can teach us, and the more our certainty and cockiness is tempered by experience.

David Elkind, professor of child psychology at Tufts University in Boston, calls this phenomenon "adolescent egocentrism." Kids believe that while parents are basically benign people who mean well, they really don't understand what it's like in the real world of adolescence. Psychologist Abraham Maslow describes this as "unconscious incompetence"—knowing so little that we don't realize how little we know. Well-meaning adults try to offer counsel to young people, but their words are drowned out by the counsel of kids' peers who are as naive as they are.

The apostle Paul warned of the impact that negative peers and bad relationships can have on decision making: "Don't be misled. Bad company corrupts good character" (1 Corinthians 15:33).

Fooled by appearances

The first bad decision in history was made by a woman who based her decision on appearances. "When the woman saw that the fruit of the tree was good for food and pleasing to the eye . . . she took some and ate it" (Genesis 3:6).

Little has changed since that first sad chapter. Today's teenagers are growing up in a culture that readily and intentionally encourages all of us to make decisions based on the way something looks. We buy cars, purchase clothing, and choose mates based on appearance. And yet, we've all heard, "You can't judge a book by its cover." Appearances can be deceiving.

Beer companies spend millions of advertising dollars annually to convince television sports viewers that sports and beer go together. We have the "Bud Bowl," the "Coors Ski Competition," and the "Bud Lite Player of the Week." Viewers don't necessarily recall a recent pro football game in Philadelphia in which drunken fans so disrupted play that alcohol has been banned at all future games in that stadium. The beer companies do not present the full picture, and we don't care to look beyond the pictures we are given.

A study done by University of Washington psychologists Elizabeth Loftus and John Palmer, and cited in *The Human Connection* by Martin Bolt and David Myers (InterVarsity Press), shows just how powerfully we are influenced by what we hear and see. Loftus and Palmer showed their test subjects a film of a traffic accident and then asked them questions about what they had seen. The subjects were divided into two separate groups. The first group was asked, "How fast were the cars going when they *smashed* into each other?" The second group was asked, "How fast were the cars going when they *hit* each other?" [emphasis mine]. The subjects in the first group gave consistently higher estimates of the impact speed than those in the second group. Even one week later, when subjects were asked whether they recalled seeing any broken glass, researchers found the same effect. There was in fact no broken glass in the accident; but those in the first group were more than twice as likely to report broken glass than those in the second group.

When we factor this data in with the fact that the average teenager is constantly being assailed with subtle and not-so-subtle visual and auditory messages from peers, music, and the media, we can begin to see how the appearances generated by those messages can affect their decision-making abilities.

What Makes for a Good Decision?

In the face of these obstacles, is it possible for teenagers to make wise decisions? Is every wrong decision necessarily a bad decision? Rich Van Pelt of Alongside Ministries draws from his extensive counseling experience to isolate three essential qualities of a wise decision. He states that a good decision first *gives adequate attention to the process of decision making*. A good decision is made after considering options, goals, and alternatives.

Second, a good decision *gives careful consideration to the consequences of one's choices*. It recognizes that choices are not made in a vacuum. Choice A will affect choice B, which will affect choice C, and so on. A wise decision factors in the reality that choosing an option will affect what further options will be available.

Third, Van Pelt considers a decision good, even if he doesn't consider it right, when the decision maker *assumes responsibility for the consequences of his or her decision*. This consideration underscores the truth that God can use wrong decisions to affect good things in our lives if we are willing to own our decisions. The only mistakes we make that we cannot learn from are the mistakes that we will not admit to. If we can help kids to accept responsibility for their decisions and their consequences, we can feel confident that they will ultimately prove to be wise decisions—because, right or wrong, they are decisions that they can learn from.

But What About You-Know-Who?

We might ask why God isn't factored into the definition of a good decision. The answer is simple. Both Christian and non-Christian teenagers can make wise and unwise decisions. It's done all the time. In using a tool like *Option Plays*, we are trying to help teenagers make better decisions. Obviously, for them to make the best decisions—Christian decisions—they need the instruction of God's Word. But they can still learn from and benefit from decisions, even if they are ignorant of God's Word, as long as they incorporate the three elements of decision making discussed previously.

It Ain't Easy

Unfortunately, describing wise decisions is much easier than making them. Too often we oversimplify the process with phrases like, "Just Say No," or

"All you have to do is . . . ." Even after the enemy had been identified, and the objectives were clear, none of Custer's options at Little Big Horn looked good. Basically, it boiled down to fight and die, try to run . . . and die, or surrender . . . and die, perhaps slowly at the hands of his captors.

That is often the way the scenario looks to kids who are in the throes of making a tough decision. If they please God, they will lose their friends. If they lose their friends, they will be lonely. If they please their parents, they may have to displease both God and their friends. And if they disobey their parents, that will surely displease God. Sometimes, you have to think that Custer had it easier. At least his options were narrowed down. And, he didn't have to live very long with the consequences of his choices!

Helping Kids Make Wise Decisions

Since it's crucial that we help our kids make wise decisions, difficult or not, what can we do to build this critical ability into them? There are four keys we must emphasize: *consider goals*, *seek God's will*, *weigh complications*, and *decide to decide*.

Consider goals

The first step in making a wise decision is giving careful consideration to one's goals. We need to help our kids to ask the question, "Where do I hope to find myself as a result of this decision?" At this stage, we are helping kids think through goals and consequences. What are their goals? Will this set of decisions lead them toward their goals?

This key helps teenagers to consider consequences and outcomes in light of their goals, hopes, and dreams. "If I want to go to medical school, I cannot afford to become pregnant in high school. If I have sex with my boyfriend, I may become pregnant. The only way to be certain I won't become pregnant is to decide not to have sex with my boyfriend."

Seek God's will

Although the first key helps kids to ask, "What do I want to do?" this key raises the question, "What does God want me to do?" But what if our students are unconcerned about God's will for their lives? That doesn't matter. Even if our kids don't care about God's will for their lives, God cares about his will for their lives. And God is God, whether our kids are concerned or not.

One of the big mistakes we make in youth ministry is growing timid at this point. We're not sure if we should tell kids what God wants them to do. Although we can't make them do what God wants them to do, we do need to make sure that we don't help them avoid or miss what God wants them to do because we were afraid to speak up.

We won't know the will of God in every situation. We need to be humble enough to admit that. But when students come to us with an issue about which God has clearly spoken, it is blatant negligence not to tell them what God has spoken.

And we can do this with confidence. Our kids already have plenty of counselors who will guide them without reference to the will of God. The very reason they have come to us is because they can trust us to share with them what God does say with reference to a situation. To be sure, we want to encourage them to open the Word and discover for themselves. And we should speak God's will with humility, gentleness, and acceptance. But we must do it. It is our God-given responsibility.

An important part of teaching this key is helping students to understand the difference between what Chuck Swindoll describes as the *precepts* of Scripture and the *principles* of Scripture. Precepts are those signposts God puts in his Word that tell us what we are and are not to do. Precepts are those obvious statements God makes about various issues: "Love the Lord your God with all your heart, all your soul, and all your mind." "Do not lie." "Do not steal." "Love your neighbor as yourself." "Do not commit adultery." "Turn the other cheek." It is clear how God's voice speaks on these issues.

But what about the questions that fall between the cracks? The Bible tells us to refrain from sexual intercourse before marriage, but what about all of the other sexual intimacy that is not excluded by that specific precept? That is where we are guided by principles. Where a specific speed limit is not posted, we might read a sign that says simply "Drive Carefully." That's a principle. It doesn't give us a specific law, but it gives us guidelines.

Unfortunately, many of us teach the precepts and neglect the principles. If we are going to help students make wise decisions, we must instruct them in both. One of the reasons this is so important is that we usually know in advance if we're going to break one of God's precepts, but we don't often know until it's too late that we've broken a principle. When do we discover that we were not driving carefully? When we have a wreck. And then it's too late.

Weigh complications

Simply knowing God's precepts and principles, however, does not mean that we apply them without regard for the context of life. I remember a girl who came to me one night after Bible study and said, "Duffy, I know you've told us that if we are Christians, we should only date Christians. Well, I've dated five of the guys in this youth group, and they were all hands! The only boy who treats me like a lady sits next to me in English class, and he says he's an atheist. Now who should I date?"

This is where *Option Plays* can be so helpful in teaching students to make wise decisions. The only way to help students work through the discipline of applying God's Word in a very complicated world is by doing it—making choices, thinking through issues, and processing why particular decisions were made.

It isn't as neat as giving out Bible verses that explain God's will, but it is the nuts and bolts of helping students apply his will in their everyday lives.

Decide to decide

The final key in teaching kids to make wise decisions is to help them come to a point of resolution. Teenagers don't usually make bad decisions because they have willfully decided to go out and sin. In most cases, they make bad decisions because they have decided nothing at all.

Few kids go out on a Friday night with the intention of breaking commandments four through seven of the Law of God. What happens goes something like this: They go to a basketball game. At the game someone suggests that they go to a movie. On the way to the movie, they meet some friends on their way to a party, and they decide to join them. When they get to the party, people are getting wasted with drugs and booze and slipping off into the bedrooms. Before they know it, these kids are making decisions they hadn't even considered.

The idea behind *Option Plays* is to help kids see that life forces us to make decisions, and those decisions have consequences. We are only kidding ourselves if we think we can withdraw from the process. Not to decide is to decide.

No Time for
Horsing Around

It's too bad that all of our decisions are not as innocuous as the second-grade horse-trading problem with which we began our discussion. Gaining or losing a few dollars isn't that big of a deal. In the real world, the stakes are higher. And the problems are a far sight more complex than anything most of us faced in the second grade.

It's serious business. Teaching kids to make wise decisions is an area in which we cannot afford to horse around.

Chapter THREE

*H*OW TO LEAD AN EFFECTIVE DISCUSSION

Chap Clark

*W*hile speaking at a ski camp a few years ago, I was asked to set up the cabin time. "The leaders have been trained and are ready to lead the discussions," I was told. "All you have to do is explain what a cabin time is and give the kids their meeting places."

After the groups had formed and begun, I sat in the back of the main meeting room where the guys' groups were gathered and glanced around to see how the discussions were going. I noticed a pattern beginning to emerge: For every group discussion, there were five leader monologues. The longer I watched, the more obvious it became that these counselors understood a "discussion" to be an opportunity for them to give another message.

Ears Open and
Mouths Closed

Unfortunately, I have found that camp experience to be all too typical. We may understand and agree with the necessity for group discussion and interaction; yet, our desire to "preach the word in season and out of season" compels us to keep hammering home our version of the truth. What we fail to realize is that words alone do not change behavior. Kids need to get personally involved with a concept before significant change can occur. And kids need the chance to struggle with new information in order to be convinced that they need the input. While solid biblical content is necessary as the foundation for understanding, time for reflection, analysis, and digestion of any content is just as essential to helping people grow.

This is especially true for today's kids. They are constantly barraged with new information, yet they have fewer and fewer opportunities to express their opinions. Rarely do friends ask questions, and many of the authorities in their lives seem to be more interested in expressing their views rather than caring about what anyone else thinks. Discussion is crucial, therefore, because it encourages kids to not only share what they know, but also what they feel—a level of sharing many adolescents rarely experience. We in youth ministry owe it to the ones we serve to program opportunities for discussion and interaction. To many kids, this will be the most valuable gift we give them—the permission to think and speak.

But there is more to leading a discussion than being committed to getting kids to talk. We must know and understand what it means to lead without stifling a group. And we must be prepared with solid content that is easy to use.

Once the content is delivered and there is a base from which to work, the hard part begins—getting the students to talk. Leading this type of discussion may come naturally to some, but for most of us it is an art to be developed. On the other hand, almost anyone can be taught to lead a discussion that gives students a sense of value as they learn about and grow in their faith.

Ground Rules for Great Discussion

Effective sharing doesn't just happen. It's a challenge to keep mistrust, domination, elitism, and other relational problems from short-circuiting the group process. The following are some ground rules to keep in mind when called upon to lead any discussion. As we take time and energy to build these tips into our leadership styles, we will develop the skills to make any discussion fun, as well as helpful, for the kids we serve.

Freedom (and safety) of speech

Evan never said much in our guys' Bible study group. He only answered those questions directed specifically to him. As the months went on, I had pegged Evan as a quiet kid. That next spring I took Evan and a few other guys (none of whom were in our Bible study) to camp. Was I in for a shock! During the cabin time, it was all I could do to keep Evan from dominating. He talked about his feelings, his family, and his faith. That night I realized that Evan didn't feel safe in our group back home. He had been forced to become shy.

For our discussion groups to be helpful to every student involved, we must be sensitive to our Evans—those kids who have a great deal to offer but, for one reason or another, don't feel free to be themselves. We must create a safe group environment, a place where kids can express their thoughts and feelings without fear of ridicule.

Trust is seldom built where relationships are absent. I had expected Evan to open up to the other guys simply because they were involved in the same youth group and went to the same school. But Evan was in a completely different crowd at school than the others, and, outside of our weekly times, never had any contact with the rest of the group. Once I discovered this, I worked harder at programming opportunities for relationships to develop within the Bible study group—an overnight for "just the guys," a dinner and ball game, impromptu movie nights. In a short time, Evan began to be himself with the group. He knew them, they were his friends, and he felt safe enough to contribute.

Small(ish) is Beautiful

Opinions vary as to the optimum size for a discussion group. Some say there should be no less than four and no more than eight; some go as high as twelve. However, we rarely have the luxury of creating the "perfect" size group. We may have fourteen students who want to stay together and only one leader who can be committed to them. Or there may only be two or three kids in a group. As much as possible, we should try to arrange groups of between four and seven kids and one to two leaders.

Mum's the Word

There must be a spoken commitment to confidentiality. If anyone feels that what they say in the group may be used against them—even in jest—it will take deep healing to restore any sense of trust.

There is an implied commitment to confidentiality in most small groups when things get "heavy." But kids can be insensitive and forgetful, and many a youth group has been torn apart by an inappropriate word or uncalled-for sarcasm. This rule should be articulated repeatedly.

Question Time

My roommate in college was one of the all-time great question askers. Dave seldom entered a discussion without first saying, "Let me ask you . . . " And never did he let you get away with a simple yes or no—he always wanted to know what you thought or felt. I guess that's why I liked being around Dave. I felt valuable with him because what I had to say mattered. And he was able to communicate that just by the way he asked questions.

How we ask a question is just as important as *what* we ask. The quickest way to ruin a discussion is to allow "yes/no/I don't know" answers to dominate. The skill is in the phrasing of the question. For example, "Do you think that Sarah was wrong in lying to her parents?" gives too much room for a "yes" or "no." On the other hand, questions like, "What alternatives did Sarah have to lying to her parents?" or "Why did Sarah feel she had to lie to her folks?" have a better chance of getting a considered response.

It is also important that we get students to talk about how they *feel* about something as well as what they think. In the above example, the way to get a "feeling" response might be: "If you were Sarah, how would you feel about having to lie to your parents?" or "How would you feel if you were Sarah's father or mother and you found out that she had lied to you?"

Silence is golden

The students in my discussion groups have become used to silence. They know it is one of my favorite tools in leading a discussion. For the new-comers, who giggle at a five-second lapse, I often explain that I like silence. It helps me to think about what the last person said and gather my thoughts for the next comment.

The obvious danger in silence is that a lull in the discussion might hurt the group interaction process. This is where the timing of a skilled leader is essential. We have to know when to let silence hang and when to interject a new thought. This takes practice, and there is no ready-made technique that fits every situation. One rule of thumb: If *we* feel like the present track is a dead end, let's move on! If we know, however, that some dead time will give kids time to think and possibly push a quieter kid to respond, we should allow ample time to respond. If we are careful observers, we can often "feel" the difference.

A little honest tension

Tension, either naturally developed or artificially introduced, is healthy for any group discussion. Without an element of struggle, there is no real point in having a discussion. If everyone already feels the same way about an issue or topic, there is no growth or movement. And without growth, a discussion is a pointless academic exercise.

Along with silence, creating a sense of tension or frustration over a certain statement or issue is a great discussion-starting tool. Most kids have been programmed to parrot easy answers to complex issues. But life is not nearly so simple, and the best way to get kids to dig deeper in discussion is to strip away their opportunity to fall back on an "easy" answer. *Option Plays* can be a tremendous catalyst for adding a controversial element to a discussion of a certain issue.

Developing An Effective Leadership Style

Sue was loving, compassionate, and a loyal friend to kids. She was also strong, opinionated, and rarely allowed room for disagreement. When the fall term began, Sue led a weekly Bible study group for a dozen senior girls who wanted to grow in their faith. Within a few months, however, the girls stopped coming to the Bible study. All the excuses sounded good, but we soon found out that, because of Sue's controlling style, the girls felt they were not free to share their honest opinions about the issues they face every day, so they dropped out of the group one by one.

Fred was hip, admired, and well liked. His Bible study reflected the guys' attitudes towards him—they were consistent and loyal. But over the course of six months, there was little growth in the lives of the guys. Most of the guys in the group dropped out of church and were becoming known as the "Christian partiers." When I visited the group to see what was going on, the problem was obvious. Fred would start with solid input, but would soon allow the guys to ignore the content and justify their attitudes and behavior while Fred just sat back looking on. Fred wanted to be liked so much that he was afraid to call them back to the Bible.

Both of these leadership styles illustrate that who we are profoundly affects how well we are able to lead discussions that help kids in their walk with Christ. Although we do need to be ourselves and lead from who we are, there are three essential qualities for an effective discussion leader:

Build relationships with every member of the group. We are responsible to make sure that every person in the group feels known and cared for. It is up to us to ensure that there is a sense of trust and safety within the group. The place to begin is in our individual relationships with every member of the group. If students know and trust us, they are far more likely to open up in the group.

Try to say something to every member of the group, even if it's only a few words, individually before and after each meeting. Whenever a comment is made during the discussion, we should affirm that student. Things as simple as a pat on the hand, a wink, a nod, or a "Thank you" will tell our kids that they are valuable and what they have to say is important.

Don't be afraid to lead. There is a delicate balance between heavy-handed leadership and allowing a verbal free-for-all. At some point, we must make sure that the group is aware of what the Bible has to say on a given issue. This is best accomplished by guiding the discussion toward a biblical perspective while drawing out the kids' own interpretations. In the end, however, if God's perspective has not clearly been brought to light, there should always be a wrap up so that kids have a foundation upon which to base their opinions.

When in doubt, listen. When I was in high school, we had a new leader in our youth group who was having a hard time breaking in with the guys. He was friendly and tried to talk when he saw us, but it seemed that every time he asked a question his eyes would wander if we took too long to answer. Before long, all we ever said to him was, "Fine," "Good," or "Okay." We didn't want to talk to him because he didn't appear to care about our responses.

It takes no special ability to be a good listener, yet the most effective youth ministry gift is listening. Anyone can learn how to listen, because listening is not so much a skill as it is a commitment—to caring enough about kids to give them our undivided attention when they speak. We can improve how we communicate that commitment, but listening is basically love and respect in action.

Listening is something we do with our bodies. The way we sit or stand when someone is talking tells them how interested we are in what they are sharing. Maintaining eye contact is essential. Whether we nod and smile with interest or impatiently stare until the person is finished speaking communicates volumes.

A good way to find out how we come across as listeners is to try this exercise. Get with two other people and have one person talk, one listen, and one observe. Then talk together about the experience, switch roles, and go through the process again. Try to help one another pick out any unnoticed "blind spots."

A practical reason for being a good listener is so we'll know what the kids are talking about when we have to jump in and clarify the direction the group is going! As the facilitator, we are often the bridge from point to point, so we must stay closely in tune with the things that have been said.

Some Closing Tips

There's much more that can be said about leading great discussions—but then we'll never get to the *Option Plays*! In closing, here are twelve practical tips to leading great discussions:

1. Sit in a circle with everyone at eye level.
2. When calling on students to share, call them by name.
3. Provide the opportunity for everyone to share without forcing anyone to share.
4. Avoid taking sides (or even revealing your opinion), especially early in a discussion.

5. Get the group to see you as a facilitator and not the supreme authority.
6. Keep any one individual from monopolizing or controlling the discussion.
7. Humor has its place, so maintain a balance—not too much to be disruptive, but not so stiff that kids don't enjoy themselves.
8. Know when to cut off a discussion.
9. Avoid leaving them with easy answers that don't relate to their world.
10. Avoid excessive harshness when you're injecting tension into a discussion.
11. Don't resolve every issue that comes up.
12. Give them something concrete to take with them after every discussion.

Chapter **FOUR**

*H*OW TO USE *OPTION PLAYS*

Noel Becchetti

*T*he beauty of Option Plays is that they're both highly creative and easy to use. The basic Option Play presents a real-life dilemma that forces your kids to decide how they would respond in that situation and the consequences that could result from their decisions.

Let's walk through a sample Option Play and see how it works:

1
COUNTDOWN TO CRISIS

Jill and her mom have been on their own for several years. Six months ago, Jill's mom remarried. Her mom, wanting to solidify the new family unit, has given Jill's new stepdad the authority to discipline Jill. Although Jill likes him and appreciates his efforts to be a father to her, she has been building up resentment toward him for what she feels is his excessive control over her life.

Tuesday night, Jill tied up the phone for more than two hours, breaking a long-standing family rule on phone use. In response, her stepfather grounded her for the weekend. Jill, not wanting to miss an important date with Bill on Friday night, asked for a different punishment. Her stepdad refused. Angry, Jill started to argue. As the discussion grew more heated, she yelled, "You're not my father! You have no right to tell me what to do!" and ran to her room.

It's now Thursday night, and Jill has a problem. Bill is calling with the details for Friday night and she hasn't told him that she can't go. She knows that Bill has already spent some money for the date and is really looking forward to their time together. She wants to go, too, and she doesn't want to make Bill angry, but she's not sure that she wants to cross her stepfather. How would her mom feel? She knows she broke a family rule, but couldn't they settle on some other punishment? Time is running out. Jill has to make some decisions.

What are Jill's options?

List options	*Best option*	*List consequences*
1		1
2		2
3		3

How to Play

1. Divide your kids into groups of three to five kids each.

2. Give each group a photocopy of "Countdown to Crisis" (it's okay with us!) or read it aloud to the whole group.

3. Give the groups eight to ten minutes to brainstorm Jill's options.

4. Bring the groups together and list all the possible options they've brainstormed on a blackboard or easel.

5. Using the diagram pictured above, have the whole group select three options that they feel Jill has available to her. List those three options on the three left-hand lines of the diagram.

6. From those three options, have the whole group select the option they feel Jill will choose. List that option on the single middle line in the diagram.

7. Now, have your whole group brainstorm three likely consequences that could result from the option they selected. List those three consequences on the three right-hand lines of the diagram. Walk the group through each consequence to its natural conclusion.

That's all there is to it! Each Option Play can generate twenty to forty minutes of lively discussion, depending on how much time you allow your kids to work with each step.

At the close of the discussion, you can wrap up with a pertinent passage of Scripture, or lead your group through a short Bible study on the topic raised by the Option Play. It's a lively, thought-provoking youth meeting all by itself.

Quick and Easy Variations

There are a number of quick and easy ways to add new elements to the basic Option Play and generate still more discussion. Here are four of the easiest:

▶ After you've worked through the consequences of the one "best" option, place your #2 option in the middle and consider its consequences; then

45

do the same with your #3 option. This helps kids to see the pros and cons of different decisions.

▸ Instead of working through the option selection with the whole group, have each small group brainstorm its own "best" option and the resultant consequences. Then bring the whole group together to share their conclusions—and watch the debate begin!

▸ When you've worked through the options and consequences for the lead character in the scenario, select one or two other key characters in the story and brainstorm *their* options. What decisions might they make? What consequences may arise? You can continue this process with all of the characters in a given scenario, if you wish. The possibilities are almost limitless.

▸ After you've traced the consequences of your "best" option, have your group brainstorm what *new* options have been created by the consequences they've listed. What options are available to Jill now? What might the consequences of *those* decisions be? You can continue this process almost forever—and it's a fantastic way to help kids see how decisions and results are interconnected.

More Variety: Audible, Substitution, and Check the Playbook

Along with the Option Plays you'll find in Chapter Five, we've developed three other variations to the original Option Play concept:

Audible (Chapter Six)

In the Audible chapter, you'll find Option Plays with an additional twist—new information about the scenario that changes the situation. After you've had your group work through the basic Option Play you've selected from Audible, throw in the audible and challenge them to brainstorm how this new piece of information might affect the options they feel are available.

Substitution (Chapter Seven)

Unlike the basic Option Plays where your kids brainstorm options for a primary character, the protagonist in Substitution is someone who has heard or seen something that they must respond to. It brings the question, "Am I my brother's keeper?" into vivid relief as your kids debate their options: Get involved? Stay out? And what will happen when either course is taken? You can play Substitution just as written.

Check the Playbook (Chapter Eight)

These Option Plays bring specific passages of Scripture (listed at the beginning of the scenario) into conflict with a real-life scenario that seems to contradict the biblical precepts.

You can either play the Check the Playbook scenarios as they're written, or delete the Scripture before letting your kids begin. Then, after they've wrestled with the situation for awhile, bring the biblical text in and ask them to brainstorm how the specific passage from God's Word might affect the options they feel are available. However you play Check the Playbook, it's a powerful learning tool.

Creative Ways to Make Option Plays *Work for You*

You can use the four varieties of Option Plays you'll find in this book in a variety of ways:

As a warm-up for your weekly youth meetings. Option Plays can be used "out of the box" to liven up a youth meeting, Sunday school class, camp, retreat, lock-in, or any other gathering you can name.

As the opening for a topical teaching series. You can pre-select specific Option Plays as "thought provokers" to get your kids wrestling with a topic that you're teaching. The handy Topical Index at the front of the book tells you which Option Plays best fit a particular topic.

As a problem-solving tool. Many of the scenarios found in *Option Plays* replicate real-life situations—perhaps even situations you're facing right now in your youth group. By leading your group through an Option Play that addresses an issue your kids are dealing with, it gives them the chance to face the issue, their possible responses to the issue, and the consequences of their responses in a safe, "laboratory" setting. They can then apply the lessons they learned from the Option Play to the real-life situation at hand, saving themselves (and you) untold possible grief and hardship.

You can see that the only limitation to using *Option Plays* is your own imagination. It's truly a creative and versatile tool to help you build better decision-making skills into your youth group.

Section Two

GAME TIME

Chapter FIVE

OPTION PLAYS

2

WHO CAN YOU TRUST?

Russ had always kept a diary. Never once in his fifteen years did it ever occur to him that someone, especially his parents, would read it. But here he is at dinner with his parents—and they have just confronted him with one of his diary entries. Russ is livid with anger. How dare his parents violate his privacy! His parents respond that if they hadn't read his diary, they wouldn't have discovered that he had a drug problem. *Maybe I do have a drug problem*, Russ thinks, *but at least I don't violate people's privacy.*

Russ's parents want him to go to a counseling program for substance abuse; *he* wants them to get counseling for their inability to respect his privacy.

What are Russ's options?

3
DIVORCE DILEMMA

Craig is discovering that, after a messy divorce, each of his parents is trying to turn him against the other. When he is at home with his mom, she picks constantly at his father. When he is with his dad, he gets the third degree about who his mom's dating. The hate is obvious, and Craig feels caught in the middle.

Last week, Craig's mom announced that her company was transferring her to another state. "Besides," she said, "then we can get away from your father." Craig was devastated. He was looking forward to spending his senior year with his friends, and he really didn't want to leave his dad.

He tried to talk to his mom about his living with his dad, even though she had custody. She would not even listen to his arguments, and eventually left the room in a huff. "We're moving in two weeks, and that's final!" were her parting words.

What are Craig's options?

4

FIRST DATE

Scott had liked Kim for a long time. Kim didn't know Scott very well, but she liked what she knew. At a party one night, Kim and Scott started talking, and finally Scott got the nerve to ask her out for the next night. Kim thought that Scott was cute and very funny, and she agreed to go out with him.

The next night, Scott showed up with a dozen roses and took Kim to one of the most expensive restaurants in town. As the night progressed, it became obvious to Kim that Scott was already way down the road with his feelings. But she barely knew him! She became extremely uncomfortable and couldn't wait to get home.

The next day, another dozen roses showed up at Kim's door, with a card: "I had a *great* time . . . Next week?"

What are Kim's options?

5

IF YOU REALLY LOVED ME . . .

Jan and John met at a party, and it was "love at first sight" for Jan. She couldn't stop thinking of John. She was thrilled when John called her the next week and asked her to go out with him. On their first date, John was the perfect gentleman—holding doors for her, asking her what she wanted to do first, kissing her lightly good-bye at the doorstep. Jan was head over heels for John.

John called her the next day and the next, and soon they were together constantly. As they spent more time together, however, Jan became increasingly aware that John wanted her to have sex with him. "It would make us even closer," John told her. Jan didn't feel it was right, but she wanted to keep John. She tried to avoid a decision although John pressed the issue with increasing urgency.

This coming weekend, John's parents are going out of town. John asks Jan to stay at his house while they are gone. Jan still feels that having sex with John is wrong, but John is starting to drop hints that if they're going to stay together, she'd better change her standards.

What are Jan's options?

6

OUT OF THE CLOSET?

Diane and Jim have been close friends since they were little. They go to the same church, their parents are friends, they have vacationed together, played together, cried together, and shared almost everything with each other.

But the kids at school are starting to talk about Jim. They're saying that he is gay. Diane defends him every chance she gets. Even though Jim doesn't have a steady girlfriend, she knows plenty of girls who like him—at least, they did until the rumors started. As the rumors grow, everyone seems to be making fun of Jim, and some kids even mock him in the halls. Jim is devastated by this, but doesn't defend himself as strongly as Diane wishes he would. Why doesn't he just get a girlfriend and put an end to the rumors?

Diane, who had never before considered that Jim could possibly be gay, begins to have her doubts. The more she listens to her friends, the less she wants to be around him. She starts withdrawing from Jim.

Jim, sensing her withdrawal, confronts Diane one day at school. He wants to know why she's turned her back on him. Diane is torn. Does she ask him directly about the rumors? What if he says that he *is* gay? What does she do then? Does she remain his friend no matter what, even if it means that she's ostracized as well?

What are Diane's options?

7

BEER BUDDIES

On an impulse, Stuart and a few of his friends from the youth group decide to have a few beers one afternoon. They do the same thing the next weekend, after playing soccer with the whole youth group, except this time they invite some of the girls along. As the weeks and months progress, drinking—"tilting a few cans"—becomes the thing to do anytime that they're together.

The youth sponsors, Bill and Charlotte, have heard rumors about drinking in the group and decide to deal with it at the next meeting. Most of the group is silent during the meeting. But a few deny any wrongdoing and refuse to acknowledge any drinking. Stuart is uncomfortable that the group is unwilling to confront the issue. He is frustrated that no one else will speak up and be honest.

What are Stuart's options?

8
WHO WILL TALK TO STEVE?

Steve is different. He is in those "special" classes, and he is very overweight. He is always alone at school, even during lunch. He doesn't have any friends, his hair is always dirty, and he never smiles. He's a real outcast.

At the church camp last weekend, Pam was overcome with the love that Jesus has for her—unconditional, overflowing, and totally free. She is still in the clouds, knowing that she is special and unique because she is a child of God, created in his image. She wants to share her newfound awareness of God's love with everyone.

Pam is sitting at lunch telling her friends about her weekend when Steve walks by. Just as he does, one of Pam's friends whispers, "Oh, no, look who's coming—it's the geek!"

What are Pam's options?

9

GOD GAMES

Carrie's parents are very religious and very conservative. They have required all their children to be active in church. Carrie's older brother, Dominick, left home when he was seventeen. He couldn't take his strict parents. Carrie wished her brother hadn't left, but she could understand. Carrie's parents refuse to talk about Dominick and view his leaving as a spiritual problem. Carrie feels bad for her parents because she knows that Dominick's rebellion has hurt them deeply.

The trouble is that, Carrie, now eighteen, cannot play the game anymore. Carrie hates her parents' church and is tired of sneaking around doing things that she doesn't think are wrong but knows that her parents would disapprove of (like dancing and going to movies). Carrie's resentment has been building. She is afraid that she won't be able to take it much longer.

Carrie believes the Bible and is committed to Christ, but not to her parents' brand of Christianity. She would like to go to another church and be honest with her parents about the way she lives, but every time she tries to talk with her parents about it they are more determined that Carrie not follow what they see as her brother's path to apostasy.

What are Carrie's options?

10
PREGNANCY PANIC

Doug's church teaches that abortion is murder, and that Christians must do whatever it takes to stop the killing. Doug starts speaking openly against abortion at school, at parties, and at any other place he can find an audience. In no time he is one of the most well-known opponents of abortion at the school.

A few weeks later, Doug goes to a game night at his youth group. While there, he strikes up a conversation with one of the cutest girls in the group, Vicki. They hit it off right away, and they spend the rest of the evening together playing, talking, and eventually cuddling. Doug drives her home and, although neither of them planned it, they have sex in Doug's car. They both feel they have blown it badly, but talk afterward and vow to exercise more control. They start dating regularly, and are able to keep their physical relationship within healthy limits.

Doug remains vocal in his anti-abortion stand at school and at church. Although Vicki likes Doug enough not to say anything, she's more ambivalent on the issue.

Several weeks after their first "date," Vicki approaches Doug at school, crying. She's discovered that she's pregnant. She's deathly afraid to tell her parents, their youth pastor, or anyone else. She wants to get an abortion. She asks Doug to help her out.

What are Doug's options?

11

CHAMPIONSHIP CRISIS

Jamie and Vince are seniors on the football team. All-League for two years running, they had become used to special treatment by the coaches, teachers, and administration. Test results always came out high enough to keep them eligible; a few cuts here and there were winked at; and drinking at school functions was somehow "overlooked." After all, Jamie and Vince are the reason the team is headed for the league championship game.

But Jamie has been having trouble with all of this for a number of weeks now. He became a Christian at a Fellowship of Christian Athletes weekend camp, and his newfound faith is beginning to cause him problems. Jamie knows the special treatment he was receiving was wrong. The question is, what should he do about it? His parents could not afford the tuition at a four-year university and Jamie has a chance at a football scholarship. With only the league championship game left, Jamie thought he could just let the issue slide, but after what happened today, it isn't going to be that easy.

Vince had convinced Jamie to cut third period with him and a couple of their buddies to help fix Vince's car. The car was easy to fix—it was out of gas—but what Vince and his buddies really wanted to do was drink . . . an entire bottle of vodka. In the past, Jamie would have joined them. He wanted to, but decided against it. When they got back to school, the news about the drinking escapade spread like wildfire.

They were all called in to the vice principal's office. Vince's buddies were suspended for two days; Jamie and Vince were warned but not suspended. Jamie knows why they weren't suspended—the championship game is tomorrow.

What are Jamie's options?

12

STRESSED OUT

Danielle finally understood why she was having headaches all the time. For years, her parents had been obsessed with Danielle "making something out of her life." Ever since she could remember, they wanted Danielle to have what they didn't have—the best clothes, private dance lessons, and, of course, the opportunity to attend the best colleges.

But Danielle is burned out on her hectic schedule. She wants to enjoy her senior year. She doesn't even care about college. Danielle wants to take a couple of years off after high school to work and travel. She's even looking into serving a term overseas with Youth with a Mission. Her parents, however, are talking Ivy League schools and dance scholarships. They have invested a lot in her future, but Danielle is beginning to feel that it is no longer *her* future. Her parents are starting to bug her about getting her college applications turned in. Time is running out.

What are Danielle's options?

13

MOM OR DAD?

Ryan has dreaded this day ever since his parents divorced. He has lived with his mother since he was eleven. He loves his mother and she is great to him, but he also loves his dad. Now that he is fifteen, he *needs* his father very much. His mother has never remarried and is still hurting from the divorce, which makes it difficult for Ryan to share his feelings about his father with her.

Ryan gets along great with his dad and his dad's new wife. The last time he visited there, his father asked him if he'd be interested in living with him for a while. Would he ever! But his mother has made it clear that such a move would be a betrayal. It would be devastating to his mother, and to their relationship. Ryan loves his mother and doesn't want to hurt her, but he really wants to live with his dad for a while. He's suffered enough pain because of the divorce. Does he have to be stuck in the middle as well?

What are Ryan's options?

14

MY FRIEND JOHN

You and John have been close friends since you were in kindergarten. Both of you have grown up in the church and are active in church and Young Life. You know John as much as you could know anyone; you have shared all your secrets. Both of you graduated from high school at the top of your class and you both have been accepted at a major university in another state.

Late one night the week before you and John are to leave for school, John comes by. He needs to talk. You drive out to your favorite talking spot. John is silent a long time; then he finally blurts out, "I'm not going to college next week. I'm moving in with a guy I met last year at a tennis tournament. Terry . . . I'm homosexual. I'm sorry I never told you about this, but you're my best friend. I didn't want to embarrass you or scare you off. But I've got to be true to who I am." John asks you to keep the conversation a secret until he's had a chance to get settled with his lover and contact his parents.

You are stunned. The emotions are overwhelming—anger, shock, hurt, empathy, confusion, depression, doubts about your Christian faith and John's. Do you keep the confidence? Talk to John's parents? Your parents? Your youth pastor? What do you say to John?

What are your options?

15

CURFEW CONFRONTATION

You have been having this same argument with your parents since your first day of high school. You've understood why they were so strict in the past, but now you are a senior. You have never been in any trouble. Your grades are excellent and you believe you have proven yourself responsible. But here you are again discussing weekend curfew.

You want to stay out past midnight for lots of reasons. All of your friends, including your girlfriend, can stay out until one A.M. on weekends. For another reason, you and your girlfriend have been going together for two years. You'd like to have a little more time alone *after* a date.

But your parents refuse to budge. They still require you to be home by eleven. You do not believe it is fair and now you have to decide what to do.

What are your options?

16
CHURCH WAR

Carol's parents have made her go to church every Sunday for as long as she can remember. They've refused to let Carol hold any job that interfered with the Sunday morning church service, and they would not even let her travel out of town for weekend volleyball tournaments.

But it's time to draw the line. Carol is sixteen, and she feels that she's old enough to make up her own mind. She doesn't want to attend church anymore. She finds the church boring and irrelevant, and the youth group is the pits. The only kids her age who are there are present only because, like Carol, they are forced to attend by their parents. Carol tells her parents she will go to church when and if she feels like it, but that she is old enough to make up her own mind.

Her parents' reaction is, to put it mildly, heated. They tell Carol that as long as she lives under their roof, she is going to church. She can make her own decisions on faith when she reaches eighteen and moves out of the house.

What are Carol's options?

17

JALOPY BLUES

Lanny has been dreaming about driving since he was in junior high school. His parents have told him that when he earns enough money to pay his auto insurance, they will consider buying him a car. They didn't say when they'd be able to get it, but now that he is a junior he knows it has to be soon.

His seventeenth birthday party was your basic item. He received the usual assortment of stuff. But as Lanny opens the last gift, he notices his dad signal to his mom with an anxious smile. Inside the box is a note telling him to look outside. The car! He knows it's the car. Lanny rushes outside to see— a rusty, dented 1974 Pontiac four-door sedan. A *four*-door?! And an ancient one to boot. Lanny is absolutely devastated. He hates the car. His parents, however, are clueless. "It was your uncle Jack's," they tell him. "The engine is in great condition and it's very safe." Lanny doesn't want to hurt his parents' feelings, but he never wants to be seen in that car.

What are Lanny's options?

18
SCARED OF STEPDAD

Christy, whose parents are divorced, has been living with her mom for a long time now. When her mom remarried, Christy was excited. She liked Tom, her new stepdad. He was friendly, good-looking, and "cool." Tom and Christy got along well, and Tom was really good for her mom. He was gentle and caring and really supportive.

Tom and her mom had been married for about seven months when Christy began to feel that something was wrong . . . or was it? Christy couldn't put her finger on anything specific, but she realized that Tom was making her feel very uncomfortable. It seemed like he was always walking by just as she was changing clothes; and when she was wearing a bathing suit his glances at her were . . . well . . . disconcerting. She had tried to discuss it with her mom, but it was obvious her mom felt that Christy was going through the normal stages of adjusting to a new stepfather. But Christy still felt uncomfortable with Tom.

She began to avoid being around him, especially when she was alone. There were times, though, when she did wonder if it was just her. She was afraid to talk to her friends because they would blab it all over. Christy could go to her youth worker or a counselor, but what would she say when they asked, "What did he do? Did he touch you?" She didn't know what to do.

What are Christy's options?

19

WILD GIRL

Teresa grew up in the poor section of town. Teresa's mother was a kid when she'd had Teresa; Teresa never knew her father. While Teresa was growing up, her mother went through a succession of men, all of whom were either drug dealers, alcoholics, or pimps. For as long as she could remember, Teresa had had to fend for herself. Teresa had learned how to survive on the streets, and she had learned how to survive the abuses of her mother's boyfriends.

By the time Teresa reached thirteen, she had had enough. She wanted out of the ghetto, out of the drugs and alcohol, and out of the gangs. She went to her mother's social worker and asked to be put in a foster home.

Now, at fifteen, Teresa has settled down. She is doing well in school and avoids any contact with her mother. Teresa's not living in the ghetto anymore, but she can't seem to escape her past. Every guy from school she goes out with assumes she is "easy"; every man (including some teachers) makes risqué remarks around her. The tough kids in school try to provoke her into fighting.

Teresa is tired of it. Why won't they let her change? To top it all off, her mother has been calling every day lately, pleading with her to come back home. Much to Teresa's amazement, she is beginning to wonder if that isn't what she should do. The whole situation seems hopeless to her.

What are Teresa's options?

20

DRUNK AND DISORDERLY DAD

Kirk is a straight-A student. He doesn't drink, smoke, or have sex. Kirk is the son that every parent wishes they had—except for Kirk's dad.

Kirk's dad is alcoholic. To make matters worse, he's verbally abusive to Kirk during his binges—calling him derogatory names, berating him for his failings, and telling Kirk that he'll never amount to anything. Kirk's mother, who has long since been browbeaten into submission, never says anything in Kirk's defense. Kirk tries to not let his father's tirades affect him too much. He doesn't want to end up like his mom.

Kirk arrives home from school one day to find a letter in the mailbox. He's been accepted to Stanford—with a hefty scholarship! Kirk floats in the door to share the great news . . . and comes face to face with his very drunk father. His father looks at him and says, "Kirk, I don't like you. I don't love you. You are a loser and you always will be a loser."

Kirk is totally devastated. He's not sure how much more abuse he can take. And is his father right? Is he really a loser, Stanford scholarship notwithstanding? He's even wondering whether it's worth going on. What's the point? Maybe he should just end it all. He doesn't know what to do.

What are Kirk's options?

21
DRIVEN TO DECEIT

It's been quite a party tonight. Most of the kids got smashed at the party—the rest came that way. Hank and his buddy, Don, came to the party sober, but Don isn't leaving that way. It's obvious that he's had too much to drink. Hank may be a partier, but he's sober tonight, and he's got enough sense to know when someone is too drunk to drive.

Hank suggests that the two of them can just drive home with somebody else. But Don is paranoid about getting his dad's car back tonight. And besides, he feels like he can drive well enough to get back home.

Hank's not excited about the idea, but he agrees reluctantly to let Don drive. At first, it looks like they might make it. Then, without any warning, Don heads for a telephone pole. Hank grabs the wheel just in time to avoid a collison. But that's it. He's not driving any further.

It's too late to get somebody from the party to drive now. Hank suggests that they call Don's dad. But the last time Don's dad caught him drinking, he put him on restriction for a month. Don is not eager for a repeat of that scene.

Don wants Hank to drive his car home. But Hank's license has been suspended for too many speeding tickets. If they should happen to get stopped, not only will Don's dad find out about the drinking, but Hank will be in big trouble with the police.

What are Hank's options?

22

HANG UP THE CLEATS?

Steve is captain of the defensive squad on the high-school football team. Although he's well liked, he's also respected for his Christian witness. Along with his teammates, he's getting pumped for the Homecoming game. Both Central High and Laney Tech, their crosstown rivals, are having great seasons, and the league championship is on the line.

As Central prepares for the game, Steve's coach begins to make some less-then-subtle suggestions that somebody ought to put Laney Tech's quarterback out of the game. He hints that a hit like that could earn the player a nomination as team MVP, a comment heard loud and clear by the college-bound players who are hoping for scholarship attention.

By Thursday practice, there is open talk on the team of a "bounty" on Laney Tech's quarterback. Steve wants to win the game as much as the next guy, and he likes to play hard-hitting football. But as a Christian, he can't condone trying to deliberately injure an opposing player.

It isn't Steve's way to talk back or oppose the coach. But he doesn't feel right about playing in a game that he knows could be marred by deliberate unsportsmanlike play. If he doesn't take a stand, his teammates will think that he condones the idea of a bounty. But if he does speak up, his teammates might think he's a quitter. And Steve already knows how the coach will react to what he'll see as insubordination. But how can he stand by while Laney Tech's quarterback is being set up for an injury?

There are fewer than twenty-four hours left before kick-off. He has to make some kind of decision.

What are Steve's options?

Chapter **SIX**

*A*UDIBLE

23

CARLA'S SECRET

Carla is outgoing, cute, and has a lot of friends. She dates occasionally, but seems to be more comfortable being with her girlfriends than with any one guy.

Carla and her best friend, Linda, decide to go with several others from their school to a Young Life camp. As the week progresses they not only have fun, but also get to know each other better than ever. One night during cabin talk, Carla doesn't get into the conversation. She sits there staring into space. All of a sudden, she starts to cry uncontrollably and runs from the cabin. Linda, not knowing what is wrong, follows her and comforts her as the crying subsides. Finally, Carla tells Linda the secret that has been killing her.

For the past eight years, Carla's grandfather has been sexually abusing her. He has threatened to kill her if she tells anyone. She feels scared, dirty, and sinful. She says she loves her grandfather, but she is *so* confused. As they walk back to the cabin, she makes Linda promise to keep this an absolute secret.

What are Linda's options?

AUDIBLE: One month later Carla calls Linda. Carla's family is going out of town for the weekend, and she wants Linda to stay overnight with her. Just as the girls are about to go to bed, Carla's grandfather shows up unexpectedly.

Now what are Linda's options?

24

WHO IS MY ELDER?

It seems that every time you go to Diane's house, her mother is screaming at the kids. You don't feel comfortable around her mother, but Diane is a good friend and you like being with her, so you put up with it.

One day after school, you and Diane are watching TV at her house. Her mom in is a worse mood than usual. She starts yelling at Diane about how she never picks up after herself. Diane ignores her and continues to watch TV. In a rage, her mom throws all the books from the kitchen table onto the floor. The only problem is, they are *your* books.

As you hurry over to pick them up, she starts in on you. This is a whole new ball game—she has never before made you the target of her abuse. You are really getting mad. You look to Diane for support, but she is still staring at the TV and apparently ignoring the whole thing.

What are your options?

AUDIBLE: Diane's mom calls your house and complains to your parents about your rudeness. Your parents, visibly upset, tell you that you're grounded for two weeks and restricted from seeing Diane indefinitely.

Now what are your options?

25

CAUGHT IN THE COOKIE JAR

It was going to be a perfect weekend—two hundred kids from several different church, Young Life, and Campus Life youth groups together in the mountains. Ted, Gary, and Bruce were ready for an awesome time.

Also on the trip were three other guys from their youth group who went to Central High, located on the "other" side of the tracks. These guys were pretty rowdy, and acted tough. Although there had never been any real problems, Ted, the unspoken leader of his trio, let Gary and Bruce know that he didn't like them very much. But when they arrived at camp, they discovered that the six of them would be sharing a cabin with two counselors from their group.

There was some mild arguing and sarcasm between the boys on Friday night, but things were basically calm. On Saturday morning, however, Ted and one of the guys from the other school got into a shouting match. The counselors were able to restore order, but the lines had been drawn.

While packing for home Sunday morning, one of the Central High guys discovered that fifteen of his CDs were missing (over $200 worth), presumed stolen. Ted had already finished packing when he heard the commotion, and when asked if he had seen anything, he just shook his head.

Gary begins to wonder if Ted stole the CDs. Ted had been talking about "getting even" after the shouting match. The more he thinks about it, the more Gary wonders if Ted is guilty. But how does he fink on one of his best friends? He'll be a traitor in Bruce's eyes. And what if he's wrong?

What are Gary's options?

AUDIBLE: The Central High guys are convinced that Ted stole their CDs. They "spread the word" to everyone who will listen and the youth pastor that they aren't coming back to the group. Ted is confronted by the youth pastor. His parents are called in. It's getting ugly. Ted continues to deny everything. A week later, Bruce pulls Gary aside and confides that he stole the CDs. He doesn't want to see Ted chopped, but he's afraid to come forward now that the whole thing's become such a big issue. "Ted will hate me," he says. "And when the Central High guys find out, they'll beat me to a pulp."

Now what are Gary's options?

26

WHAT WILL WE DO WITH KARLEEN?

Karleen was popular, attractive, and well liked by both girls and guys. There was only one problem: Karleen didn't believe she was attractive, popular, or well liked. She was very insecure and had often confided in her friends that she had considered suicide.

As Karleen's insecurities increased, it grew more difficult for her friends. She was always getting her feelings hurt, always wondering if her friends still liked her, and always having a crisis. As a result, Karleen created the very problems she worried about.

You have been Karleen's friend ever since elementary school. Now, as a junior, you want to work on your own friendships and your own relationships, but you are worried Karleen will not be able to handle your backing off of a close friendship.

What are your options?

AUDIBLE: You come home from school one afternoon to find your mother beside herself. Karleen *has* attempted suicide. It was unsuccessful, but now she's in the hospital recovering from an overdose of pills.

Now what are your options?

27

MEXICO MADNESS

Your youth group was headed for Mexico Easter week to build houses for the poor. Your boyfriend, Ken, didn't want to go. He wanted to spend Easter week at his parents' beach house in Hawaii. But at your urging, he reluctantly decided to go. You thought it would do him good because he has been raised in such a wealthy environment.

But never in your wildest dreams did you expect Ken to respond the way he did. You expected him to barely endure the week . . . but Ken was shocked, overwhelmed, and then angry. He had never seen such poverty. Ken immersed himself in the week, building houses at a feverish pitch. Later that week, Ken told you that he had decided to sell his car, take the money from the sale, and give it to the poor. He also told you that he intended to encourage his parents to divert most of their wealth to the poor when he returned home.

In your heart, you wondered if Ken was overreacting. And, quite honestly, you were worried. You like Ken's wealth. You like going to nice places in his nice car. You've enjoyed helping the poor in Mexico one week a year, but you're not sure that being a Christian means throwing your whole life away.

It's now a month after the Mexico trip, and you realize that Ken was not kidding. He has sold his car. He and his parents are getting into major fights over Ken's insistence that they change their lifestyle. Ken thinks you are in total support of what he is doing. He wants to get together and talk about the situation.

What are your options?

AUDIBLE: When you get together for your conversation with Ken, he confronts you on *your* priorities. He reminds you that you're the one who first opened his eyes to the real needs out there, and wants you to join him in living a more biblical lifestyle.

What are your options now?

28

AIDS NIGHTMARE

Graham has heard about AIDS for years now, but he has never considered it a problem for him or his family. Graham's mom and dad are very active in church, very public in their commitment to Christ, and happy in their marriage. It never occurred to Graham that AIDS would ever be a problem for him.

Now Graham is sitting in his living room, but it feels like he's on another planet. His mother and father are telling him that they have AIDS. They tell him that his dad contracted AIDS from a blood transfusion and unknowingly passed it on to his wife. They're "innocent" . . . yet the innuendos and fear will come nonetheless.

Graham's entire world is crumbling before him. How could two good Christian parents get AIDS? Why would God let that happen? It won't be long before the entire town knows. How can Graham ever show his face at school or church?

What are Graham's options?

AUDIBLE: Later, Graham's parents reveal that during a rocky time in their marriage some years before, Graham's dad visited a prostitute. She apparently passed the AIDS virus to him, and he to his wife. This was actually how they contracted the virus.

Now what are Graham's options?

29

DRUG DEALERS

Tim and Darlene are Christians. Both are active members of Young Life, both are from good homes . . . and both are drug dealers. They don't believe that they are doing anything wrong. They're only selling marijuana, which is about the same as alcohol, isn't it? They believe that the kids are going to buy the marijuana anyway, so it's not as if they're creating new drug addicts. And they don't waste their profits on fancy cars and flashy clothes. They're saving for their college educations.

But Tim and Darlene have a problem—Keith, their Young Life director. He's heard the rumors, and he's standing in front of them asking them if the rumors are true. He says if they are, he is going to the police. Tim and Darlene are scared, but somewhat amused because a number of the kids who buy from them do it at the Young Life club meetings. They also deal to the daughter of a very prominent pastor in town.

Tim and Darlene tell Keith that they do deal drugs, that they don't think it's wrong, and that if Keith says anything, they'll reveal some interesting names from their customer list. Keith doesn't miss the implied threat.

What are Keith's options?

AUDIBLE: During his confrontation with Tim and Darlene, they tell Keith that one of the kids they are selling pot to is his son.

Now what are Keith's options?

30

DATING DILEMMA

Fred has been an asset to the youth group ever since his family joined the church last summer. He's been a regular attender, has provided leadership in the group, and is friendly and outgoing. He's also the only black kid in the group.

Lately, Fred has been spending a lot of time with your best friend, Karen. They really seem to like each other . . . and now Karen has come to tell you that Fred has asked her out. Karen's parents went through the roof when Karen told them about her date with Fred. They absolutely forbid her to go out with him. When Karen asked them how they could justify their position as Christians, they grounded her for a week.

Karen wants to go out with Fred, and she asks for your help. Karen wants you to "invite" her out to the movies on Friday night . . . where she will rendezvous with Fred.

What are your options if you are Karen's friend?

AUDIBLE: Karen wants you to invite her out . . . but for a double date. Fred's friend, Eric, is in town. Karen tells you that Eric is a great guy and a lot of fun—but he's also black. If your parents ever find out that you dated a black guy, there will be hell to pay.

Now what are your options?

31
FAITHFUL FRIEND?

Elaine and Sherry had been friends for a long time. Elaine was well aware of the drug problems in Sherry's past, but Sherry had insisted that that was all behind her. For Elaine, being a true Christian friend meant supporting and trusting someone even if their past hadn't been that great.

But that loyalty was put to the test when Sherry announced her plans to run for president of the church youth council. Elaine wanted to support her friend, but she wasn't sure that this was what Sherry or the youth group needed right now. Several youth group members felt that Sherry's past made her a less than appropriate candidate for a leadership role in the youth group. Elaine felt that the last thing Sherry needed at this point in her life was more responsibility and pressure. She felt that Sherry needed to focus on her personal walk with the Lord.

But if Sherry wanted to be president, shouldn't Elaine be loyal? How might Sherry take it if her best friend didn't support her trying to serve the Lord?

What are Elaine's options?

AUDIBLE: Three months after Sherry's election victory, Elaine hears rumors that Sherry is still using drugs. When Elaine confronts Sherry, Sherry admits that once, but just once, she has done drugs. She knows that it was wrong, has repented for her sin, and feels that God has forgiven her and forgotten about it.

What should Elaine do? Does she tell the youth group? Does she tell Sherry that she can no longer support her for any kind of leadership role? Or does she just keep quiet about the one mistake?

Now what are Elaine's options?

32

FORBIDDEN FELLOWSHIP

Karen's family is Jewish. When she became a Christian, there were some major problems at home. The day her parents forbade her from having anything further to do with the church youth group was one of the saddest days of her life.

She wanted to obey her parents because she knew that was an important part of her new commitment to God and his Word. But she also knew that the youth-group Bible study had been a spiritual lifeline to her. Cutting her off from that teaching and fellowship would be like pulling the plug on her spiritual life-support system.

What are Karen's options?

AUDIBLE: Karen's dad has been doing some serious thinking about his own faith. Two months after Karen came to her initial decision for Christ, she overhears a conversation one night between her parents. Her dad tells her mom that he has been watching Karen's life and that it was causing him to do a lot of thinking about his own life. He says that he dares not reveal any of this to Karen because she's "already become some kind of Jesus freak. If she knows about this, she'll really start pushing to go back to that youth group." He swears Karen's mom to secrecy.

Now what are Karen's options?

33
BETTING ON A FRIENDSHIP

John and Tim had been friends all through junior high and high school. They had done everything together, from serving on the student council to working on the youth group summer mission project. A few months ago, one of the guys at the burger joint they both worked at had offered them a chance to buy into the weekly football pool. It would be a way to add a little fun and excitement to the weekend. John and Tim both anted up.

As the season went on, John became worried that Tim was gambling more money than he should. He was starting to bet the bulk of his paycheck on the weekend line-up. Tim had even gotten the friend at work to put him in contact with a bookie who could open him up to a little more "action."

After the first week of the playoffs, Tim comes to John needing a favor. He has had some bad luck over the last few weekends and has fallen behind financially. He's beginning to get some pressure from the bookie to pay up—fast. The bookie had made it clear that there would be phone calls to Tim's youth pastor, school principal, and his parents if he didn't pay up.

John isn't sure what to do. He's beginning to wonder if he really would be doing Tim a favor by helping him pay off his debts. On the other hand, Tim needs help. There's a friendship on the line here.

What are John's options?

AUDIBLE: Tim has lied to John about the size of his gambling debt. It is far bigger than he has said. Tim is getting some serious threats from the bookie—he's talking about really hurting Tim if Tim doesn't come up with the money. Tim is really scared.

Tim feels the only way he can get enough money to pay off the debt is to borrow money for a big bet on the upcoming Super Bowl game. He asks John for the loan, telling him that this is his one chance to get out of the gambling mess altogether.

Now what are John's options?

34

BEING A GOOD "WITNESS"

Jeannie was on her way with Brad to visit one of the youth group kids in the hospital. She had been afraid to drive downtown because of the extra traffic, and Brad was one of those youth workers who was always there when you needed him.

Unfortunately, as they were driving through the hospital parking lot, Brad cut too close to one of the parked cars. He clipped its right side and made a serious gash in the side of the car, smashing the tail light in the process.

Brad stopped immediately, got out, and walked over to the car he'd hit. It was quiet—they were the only ones in the lot. Jeannie figured that Brad was leaving a note to tell the owner of the car what had happened.

Brad returned to his car, got back in, and proceeded to park at the other end of the lot. Jeannie couldn't be sure . . . but *had* Brad left a note for the other driver? She really hadn't seen him do it. Was Brad going to sneak away from the accident? That wasn't right. But Jeannie felt sort of responsible for the whole thing. After all, Brad was there only because she'd asked him to drive her to the hospital.

Jeannie had almost forgotten about the incident when the police stopped by the church later that week. It turned out that someone else had witnessed the accident out of one of the hospital windows. They'd written down the license number of Brad's car and given it to the police. But when the police visited Brad at his church office, he denied that he'd been involved in the accident. The police asked Brad if he had any witnesses to support his story . . . so he gave them Jeannie's name.

Now the police investigator has made an appointment to see Jeannie the day after tomorrow.

What are Jeannie's options?

AUDIBLE: The day before her appointment with the police, Brad calls Jeannie. He is really worried about what might happen if the police find out that he really did hit that car. Not only will he be in trouble for lying to the police investigators, but if he has to pay for the damages, it would be financially devastating. His car insurance only covers personal liability— he's responsible for all collision expenses. He's not making much at the church, and if he was hit with a major repair bill, he might have to leave youth ministry to take a higher-paying job. He admits to Jeannie that he was wrong to leave the scene of the accident and lie to the police, but he can't see the point of losing his ministry just because of one dumb mistake.

Now what are Jeannie's options?

35
RETREAT PROTEST

The annual winter retreat was the high point of the year for your youth program at First Church. Kids would invite their non-Christian friends to come, and there would always be a number who would make an initial commitment to Christ. It was a fun and powerful way for your kids to reach out to their friends at school.

But this year, there is a growing tension. Tony, your youth council president, took part in an urban outreach project the previous summer. That experience gave him a new perspective on the poor, and how folks in the suburbs—and youth groups in suburban churches—spend their money.

Tony realizes that the poorer kids at his school will never be able to go on the youth group ski trip, and it really bothers him. He feels that it is selfish for the group to plan an expensive trip when it will exclude so many kids. To Tony, that doesn't sound like something Jesus would do. He's beginning to voice his concerns to other kids in the group. Some of the kids are agreeing with him; others are violently opposed. It's beginning to polarize the group.

What are your options?

AUDIBLE: Tony won't drop the issue, and things are heating up. There is growing talk of a boycott. One night after youth group, several of the kids get into a shouting match. Tony accuses you of planning a retreat that is financially out of reach for poorer kids because the church doesn't really want those kids in the group. Things are getting so bad that the church board suggests you consider cancelling the retreat this year.

Now what are your options?

Chapter **SEVEN**

SUBSTITUTION

36
MISSIONARY DATING

Ron and Mary have been dating for six months. Now that the two of them are getting more serious, Mary's parents are growing concerned about the relationship. It's not that they don't like Ron—they do. But they, along with Mary, are committed Christians. Although Ron and his family attend the same church, and Ron has been a faithful member of the youth group, he has said bluntly that he is not a Christian and is not convinced that the Christian faith is any more valid than any other belief system. Although this bothers Mary, she is convinced that through their relationship, she can help him come to know Christ.

Mary's parents don't see it that way. They think Mary is naive. In fact, they think Ron's attendance at youth group has a lot more to do with Mary than it has to do with any fledgling interest in Jesus. They tell Mary that, with the exception of youth group meetings, she is to stop seeing Ron.

Mary relates this last pronouncement with a rush of tears. Mary has been your best friend for years, and you've been going to the same church since you were in grade school. Mary knows her parents mean well, but she feels that they just don't understand. And she really loves Ron. "He treats me wonderfully and is a perfect gentleman," she sobs. "He says that I can be as religious as I want. How could such a good relationship be wrong in God's eyes?"

Mary wants to keep seeing Ron. She asks you to let her and Ron use your house for a meeting place, so they can continue to meet without her parents finding out. And she begs you to keep the whole thing a secret, especially from the youth pastor.

What are your options?

37

WASTED WITNESS

Your friend Sue doesn't consider herself a drinker. She only goes to parties because her friends enjoy them. As a Christian, Sue feels it is important to spend time with her nonbelieving friends, and parties are a great way to do that.

One Friday night, Sue goes to a large party and has a few beers with her friends from school. Before she realizes it, Sue can hardly walk. Right about then, you show up at the party. As you go over to Sue, you can see that she is drunk—and sharing her faith in Christ with some kids as drunk as she. You're appalled that Sue is drunk, but you're not sure what to do. Do you confront her? Drag her home? Let her go ahead and share with them? Talk with them yourself?

What are your options?

38

SWORN TO SECRECY

Your friend Jeremy is the son of one of the most influential families in the church. He shows up one Sunday morning with a black eye. He shrugs it off, saying that he bumped it. No one presses him and it is soon forgotten.

While playing basketball two weeks later, Jeremy takes off his shirt to be a "skin." His shoulder is a mass of deep purple bruises. After the game, you drive Jeremy home and ask him about his arm. Jeremy pauses, begins to say something, and then yells, "It's none of your business! Forget it, will ya?!" Hurt that Jeremy was so angry, you decide to back off and not see him for a while.

A month later, you and Jeremy are back on good terms, and you're on your way to pick him up for youth group. As you approach his front door, you hear loud yelling. Looking through the picture window, you see Jeremy being knocked flat by his father. What do you do? You finally ring the doorbell. Jeremy's father answers the door and acts as if nothing has happened. Jeremy comes out a few minutes later with a rising welt on the right side of his face. You ride to youth group in stony silence.

What are your options?

39

KATY'S COMEUPPANCE

You know Katy from youth group. Outgoing and attractive, Katy likes to date. She is not really interested in being tied down to one guy, but she enjoys having lots of guys interested in her. You know this from experience, since you're one of the guys she has dated and dropped.

Robbie is a popular, athletic, and good-looking senior. He's well aware of Katy's dating history, and sees her as a tremendous challenge. Robbie makes it his ambition to get Katy to fall for him, sleep with him (he has heard that she is a virgin), and then dump her.

Katy, while moderately experienced, is totally naive about Robbie's intentions. He treats her better than any guy she has ever dated. He is polite, considerate, and caring. He surprises her with flowers and notes. She has finally found a guy worth committing to.

One day at school, you're hanging with a group of Robbie's friends when you overhear them bragging about Robbie's plans to "teach Katy a lesson." You haven't talked to Katy since she dropped you, and you're still smarting from the experience. But you don't like what you're hearing from Robbie's friends.

What are your options?

40

AVERAGE ANXIETY

Clint is lying on his bed, staring at the ceiling. He has just returned from youth group where once again he has heard how Christians are outgoing, talented, and the best at whatever they attempt. Great. Clint knows he is none of those things.

He's not ugly, but he's no pin-up boy. His grades? Bs and Cs . . . and that's if he really studies. Clint knows he's just an average guy destined to live an average life. Even when he sins, it's average.

Clint is ready to quit the youth group and drop out of church. It's obvious by the parade of Christian football players, Christian beauty queens, and Christian corporate giants that he's been exposed to over the years that Christianity is not for average guys like Clint. Clint thinks he is living up to his potential, which is average. Apparently you can't do and be a Christian, so Clint figures he might as well chuck it all.

You're shocked by Clint's call. He's one of your buddies in youth group, but you never suspected that he was so discouraged. As he pours out his frustration, you feel more and more at a loss.

What are your options?

41
MANHANDLED

Tammy is a very attractive girl who always has plenty of guys wanting to go out with her. Her latest boyfriend, Reggie, is gorgeous, and she really likes him. Their first few dates were great. The fourth date, though, was more like a wrestling match. Tammy was used to wrestling matches, but normally it only happened once. Then the guy got the message or they got lost. But Reggie was different. He kept pushing and pushing. She kept resisting, but it got more and more difficult. She pleaded with him to stop, but he wouldn't. They had sex.

At first Tammy felt guilt for letting things go so far. She blamed herself. She was so ashamed that she didn't tell anyone about it—not her best friend and certainly not her parents. She broke off the relationship with Reggie, but the incident still haunted her. Then she saw a television show on date rape and realized what had happened to her. Reggie had raped her! It was not her fault.

She confronted Reggie, but all he did was laugh. "Hey, babe," he told her, "you wanted it and you know it. Come on, don't you remember what you wore that night?" She cringed at the thought—she'd worn a low-cut blouse, and her miniskirt *had* been one of her smallest.

She went to a lawyer friend of her father's to see if he could help her. The lawyer was sympathetic, but warned Tammy that because she had waited so long to press charges, Reggie could make her look bad in court. He could ruin her reputation and she could still lose the case.

Nonetheless, Tammy can't let go of her struggle. She was *raped!* Finally, she comes to you—the youth pastor at her church, although she's not what you'd call a member. She hardly comes to youth group and attends church sporadically at best. You don't even know Tammy that well—except that she's got a reputation with the guys in the group as a sexy flirt. Tammy is sitting across from you, tears pouring down her face as she recounts her story. She still hasn't told her parents.
What are your options?

42

A CHEESEBURGER AND A SMALL THREAT

Billy and Chad were having lunch in a fast-food restaurant when they heard some guys talking at the table across the aisle. And what they heard wasn't good.

From what they could pick up, it had something to do with the gangs. Gang rivalries weren't anything new around their area. But what these guys were talking about sounded like life . . . and maybe death. And to complicate matters further, they knew the guy who was being discussed. Marty Pitts wasn't any angel, but he was a guy they were friendly with at school.

Chad and Billy couldn't just act like they hadn't heard anything. To ignore what they had heard would almost make them accomplices to assault, or maybe murder. But they also knew that warning Marty might not be enough to save him. And if anyone should find out that Billy and Chad had talked, *they* could be the topic of the next luncheon meeting.

What are Billy and Chad's options?

43

PARALYSIS PRISON

Shauna lay still in her hospital bed. She had never known such depression until now. She doesn't want to see her family or friends—including you, her longtime boyfriend.

Until six weeks ago Shauna's life was like Disneyland. She had everything going for her—good looks, great mind, super family. Then her car was hit head-on. She woke up paralyzed from the waist down. The doctors tell her she will never walk again.

Shauna remembers her first thoughts: "No boyfriends. No marriage. No sex." She remembers all the kids she knows in wheelchairs. Everyone is nice, too nice. She remembers all the handicapped jokes. People don't really like handicapped people, they just put up with them. She remembers a weekend retreat she was on recently. Every time the girls decided to go somewhere, they would forget to ask Deborah to go with them. They didn't mean to forget her, they just did. Of course, Deborah was in a wheelchair.

She knows that you're going to drop her and date other girls. After all, who wants to date a cripple? Every time you try to see her, she turns her face to the wall and starts to cry.

You're trying to fathom all of this as you sit next to Shauna's bed. You love Shauna, but you're stunned by this terrible turn of events. Should you stick with her? Is it okay to start dating other people? Do you have a Christian duty toward her? If so, what is it? You don't know what to do.

What are your options?

44

AM I MY BROTHER'S KEEPER?

It's not as if you were snooping. You were just opening your locker, getting some books, and there it was. On the floor in front of the locker next to yours was a carefully scripted, neatly written note dated for the next day. Some of the sentences didn't make sense. There were a couple of weird quotes that seemed like they might be from some song. But one thing was clear: Whoever wrote this note was writing it to explain why he was ending his life, and he hadn't intended it to be found— at least not today. Or had he? You can't figure out who wrote the note. You know all your locker mates, but you can't recognize the handwriting on the note.

Do you turn the note in to the principal? Will he call in everybody who has a locker in that area? That could make you *really* popular. What if the note's just a bad joke? Or what if the kid has changed his mind? If you turn in the note, you're going to get this guy in such a huge mess, it may backfire and make him do something crazy.

Maybe you should just act as though you didn't see the note. But what if you do ignore it and then find out tomorrow that some kid committed suicide?

What are your options?

45

UNDERCOVER AND OVERHEARD

Tom was sitting outside Mr. Jenkins' office for an appointment one morning when he overheard a conversation between Mr. Jenkins and Mr. Benson, the school's security officer, about an undercover narcotics operation at the high school. Tom might have been able to act like he hadn't heard anything if he hadn't heard the name of Chip Feester. Everybody knew that Chip Feester was dealing drugs around the school.

Tom didn't approve of Chip's drug dealing, but he tried to look at Chip as just another person who was hurting and lonely and needed Jesus. He couldn't see Chip's sin as any worse than the next guy's. And Tom had been spending time witnessing to Chip. Chip had approached him a few weeks back with some questions about God. Tom felt like he was beginning to make some headway. It seemed that Chip might be on the threshold of a new relationship with Christ.

Should he warn Chip about the narcotics operation? Wouldn't he be obstructing justice if he exposed the plan? But could he stand by and watch Chip get trapped? But drug dealing was wrong. If Chip was guilty, didn't he deserve to be caught?

What are Tom's options?

Chapter **EIGHT**

CHECK THE PLAYBOOK

46

TESTIMONY TURMOIL

1 Thessalonians 2:2–13

Bill is part of a leadership team of students who go out from his church on a regular basis and lead retreats for other youth groups. They use drama, music, small groups, and personal testimonies. God has been using their efforts in dramatic ways. It seems that kids are more willing to listen to kids, maybe because they know they can trust them to shoot straight.

It has been a very special weekend. On Friday and Saturday nights, Bill stayed with Jim, one of the kids at the host church. By Saturday night, Jim was asking Bill some very tough questions. It was obvious that he was getting serious about making some kind of commitment.

But there was one hitch. Jim confided to Bill that he's been doing drugs, and he's not sure that Jesus could help him deal with his desire to get high. Bill assured him that Jesus can do anything. Jim replied, "How do you know? Have you ever done drugs?"

Looking back, it was a stupid thing to do. But without thinking, Bill answered yes. He hadn't really done drugs, but Bill knew that if he had said no, that would have ended the conversation right there.

Jim started pressing for details. Bill didn't want to turn around and say, "Oh, I didn't really use drugs. I just said that." So Bill kept adding more and more details, all of them untrue. *I'll be out of town tomorrow*, he thought. *Jim will never know that I lied.* The conversation finally ended around two o'clock in the morning when Jim prayed to receive Christ. It was fantastic!

It seemed like a miracle in the making—until the Sunday school meeting later that morning. Jim began sharing how he had accepted Christ the previous night. It wouldn't have been possible, he added, without Bill's help. Then he said, "I need to confess something. I've been doing drugs for the last year. I know it's wrong. But last night, Bill shared with me how the Lord had helped him quit doing drugs, and I know now that Jesus can help me too."

Whoops. Every head in Bill's youth group spun in his direction. Some of them were thinking, "Bill did *what*?!" Others, who knew it wasn't true, were thinking, "Did Bill actually lie to that guy?" It was not a pleasant scene.

What should Bill do? Should he stick to his story? Should Bill confess that he won Jim to Christ with a lie? And what if Jim finds out? What might that do to his fragile new commitment to Jesus?

What are Bill's options?

47
PUNKER PARANOIA
1 Timothy 4:12

Brenda, Brad, Darrell, and Trish are all longtime friends, part of the youth group—and have all become punkers. The reaction has been swift and universal. Their parents, the kids at school, and the youth group have all been, let's say, less than ecstatic with the new punker quartet. Worst of all, nobody takes them seriously.

The punkers know they are considered weird, but they want to continue being a part of the youth group. In fact, they believe the youth group is being unchristian because Christ teaches that believers should accept people where they're at. The punkers have decided to confront the youth group with what it is they are doing—but they don't know how to go about it.

What are their options?

48

SATURDAY NIGHT AT THE MOVIES
Matthew 5:27–30; Romans 12:1–2; Philippians 4:8

Saturday nights can get incredibly boring, especially if you are a Christian who doesn't feel right about going to parties where there's a lot of drinking and drugs.

Phil, Jerry, and Stan—three leadership guys from First Church—have always had a hard time trying to figure out what to do on Saturday nights. More often than not they've ended up going to the movies, and many of the movies they've seen are R-rated.

They hadn't thought much about this until the winter ski retreat. The speaker, in the middle of one of his talks, threw out the comment that "a good Christian young person would never go to an R-rated movie!" When they got to the cabin that night, Phil and Jerry were angered by that comment. They told their cabin leader that they thought the speaker was out to lunch. "Everybody goes to R-rated movies. And what else is there to do on a Saturday night?"

Since the retreat, though, Stan has been bothered. He feels convinced that, because of the language, nudity, and violence found in so many R-rated movies, he shouldn't go see them anymore. Yet here he is, driving around with Phil and Jerry on Saturday night, trying to figure out what to do. Finally, Phil and Jerry suggest that they might as well go to the movies.

What are Stan's options?

49

TAKING ON THE TEACHER
1 Peter 2:21, 23; 3:15–17

Mr. Jones is Todd's biology teacher. He loves to make disparaging comments about the intelligence of anyone who believes in God. As Mr. Jones begins a unit on evolution, he is in rare form as he rails against "those Bible beaters." Most of the kids enjoy hearing Mr. Jones' tirades, and they encourage his outbursts.

Todd has been in this class all semester without anyone knowing that he is a committed Christian. He's kept his mouth shut so far through Mr. Jones' "cut" sessions against the Christian faith, but it's beginning to get to him. Today, Todd feels like he's hitting his limit. The more Mr. Jones spouts, the angrier Todd gets.

What are Todd's options?

50

YE MUST BE BORN AGAIN

1 Timothy 4:7–5:2; Colossians 3:20; 4:5

Jeff had gone to church all his life. He was confirmed in ninth grade, was active in youth group, and grew up believing that religion is a good thing.

In the fall of his sophomore year, a few of Jeff's friends got him to come to a Christian club at his high school. In November, Jeff went to a camp with his club and heard about Jesus in a way he had never heard before. Jesus became real in a new way for him. When the speaker invited everyone to give their lives to Jesus, Jeff did, and he knew deep in his heart that he was a different person. He was a Christian.

When Jeff got home, he burst in the door and poured out his experience to his parents and two sisters. The more he talked, the more he encouraged them to realize that they needed to become Christians like he had. Before they could reply, he ran out the door—he couldn't wait to get to youth group to let them know what had happened to him.

The church Jeff's family attended believed that knowing Jesus was a process that included education, exposure to important social issues, and spiritual milestones like confirmation. When Jeff started talking about his conversion, his youth minister told him that he already was a Christian. "Those people are trying to get you to become something you already are!" Jeff tried arguing with him, but because his youth leader was better prepared on this issue, Jeff just got mad and frustrated. He finally left, telling his youth pastor, "You just don't understand!"

When Jeff got home, his parents were fuming. How dare he accuse them of not being "real" Christians? Who did he think he was, trying to preach to them? While Jeff was at youth group, they had called his club leader and let him know that Jeff would not be allowed to come to club anymore. They finished the discussion by grounding him for two weeks.

What are Jeff's options?

51

FIGHT NIGHT
Romans 12:16–21

Dan, a reserve guard on North High's basketball team, has never been a fighter. The only time he was ever in a fight was in a sixth-grade basketball game. As a Christian, he believes that Jesus told him to love his enemies.

One day during lunch, Dan was in the gym shooting some baskets by himself. Some guys came in whom he had seen around but didn't know. The ball bounced off in the direction of the group of guys, and Dan asked them to toss the ball to him. Instead, one of the guys gave Dan a hard look and threw the ball to the far end of the gym. Dan gave him a disgusted look, then turned to get the ball. The kid who threw the ball started for Dan, challenging him to a fight. Dan at first ignored him, and when he couldn't, he told the guy he didn't want to fight. "Chicken . . . wimp . . . geek," they taunted Dan. Dan just turned and left. As he was leaving, the kid yelled out, "I'll meet you in the parking lot after school, chicken!"

It took less than an hour for the whole school to be buzzing with the news of the upcoming fight. Dan didn't know what to do. He was afraid, and he was mad. He also knew that he was stronger than he looked and felt like this guy needed to be taught some manners.

What are Dan's options?

52

THE PARENT TRAP
Romans 12:16–21

Debby was eighteen years old and ready to get out of the house. Her mother and dad were extremely protective. There was good reason. Debby's mother had been a wild woman in high school—in fact, Debby was the result. Debby had tried hard to please her parents. Her youth pastor taught that the Bible tells us we should honor our fathers and mothers. She was not the kind to argue or resist . . . until now.

Debby was looking forward to going away to college in a few months. She had been accepted at a major university in another state. But tonight, her parents announced at dinner that they wanted Debby to go to the local junior college. They gave Debby an ultimatum—stay at home and attend the local JC for two years, or pay every dime of her education costs. They promised that if she stayed, they would pay for any college she wished to attend.

But Debby wondered if they really would. Debby's mother has been getting more protective. She has been even getting paranoid, accusing Debby of being a slut because she came home an hour late on a date. Debby is worried that they might try to keep her home forever.

What are Debby's options?

53

TO HEAR OR NOT TO HEAR?

1 Corinthians 10:31–33; Ephesians 4:29

It is one of those lunch table conversations in which everyone is sharing their favorite stories. Some of the humor is pretty raunchy. At Bible study last week, there was a big discussion about appropriate language and humor. You're feeling like the Lord wouldn't be laughing if he were sitting with you right now.

If you laugh along with everybody else, does that mean that you approve of what's happening? It would be easy for the guys to take it that way. On the other hand, there's no reason why being here means that you have to join in. And if you leave the table now, you can forget about talking to these guys about stuff that really does matter.

Your youth minister ended last week's Bible study with the admonition: "Just ask, 'What would Jesus do?' " Well, what *would* he do?

What are your options?

54

TO TELL THE TRUTH
Ephesians 4:25ff; Zechariah 8:16

By the look of your dad as he came in the door from work, you could tell it had been one of those days. The phone rings, and you answer it. It's your dad's boss, and he sounds upset. He says he needs to speak to your dad, and it's urgent.

With your hand cupped over the receiver, you tell your dad that his boss is on the phone. He just waves his hand and mumbles, "Tell him I'm not home yet."

You should probably just help your dad out. But in your morning devotions, you read about the importance of always telling the truth. But if you do tell the truth, your dad will get mad—and as upset as he is, he might say something to his boss that he'll regret.

The same Bible that says to tell the truth also instructs you to obey your parents. And the boss isn't going to hold the phone forever.

What are your options?

55

CRISIS IN BLACK AND WHITE

Galatians 3:28; 1 Corinthians 10:23–33; 1 Corinthians 8:9–13;
1 Corinthians 9:1–5; 1 Timothy 4:12

First Church sends a youth witness team out every summer. They tour several hundred miles on bicycles, stopping and witnessing in small communities along the way. They'll do everything from leading a three-day Vacation Bible School for children to repainting a church. It's intense work, but the time spent together in service brings them closer in their relationship to the Lord and with one another.

But things are getting sticky this summer. Sal and Jenny began dating at the beginning of the tour. That wouldn't usually be a problem—except that Sal is white and Jenny is black. In a number of towns along their route, the local people noticed their relationship and were bothered by it. Resentment is building within some members of the group who feel that Sal and Jenny's relationship is hindering the group's ministry. They feel that interracial dating is becoming more of an issue than Jesus.

To Sal and Jenny, that's just the point. Their relationship is a powerful testimony to the fact that all are one in Christ. And some of their ministry teammates support their view.

Tensions are getting worse by the day. Finally, three of the team members approach you, the leader of this year's team, at breakfast. They feel that something needs to be decided so that group unity can be restored.

What are your options?

56

TOO CLOSE FOR COMFORT
Romans 14:13; 1 Timothy 4:12

Bob, Tim, Carolyn, and Alycia, all officers on the church Youth Council, were planning to go away for the weekend to a Christian concert in a town about five hours' drive away. They were going to stay in two separate hotel rooms to guard against any hanky-panky. It really was all very harmless — or so they thought.

But when John, their youth minister, got wind of the trip, he hit the roof. He called Bob in to tell him that their plans showed very poor judgment. Setting up an overnight trip like that was not only irresponsible, it was stupid. "What are people supposed to think when they hear about it? It'll blow your witness!"

Bob got angry. He accused John of not trusting him. It was nobody's business, he replied, whether he and some Christian friends went away for the weekend. That was between them and God. Maybe this was a chance to show their friends that guys and girls can get together for a great time and not have to have sex. If John didn't trust them, that was his problem.

That wasn't the reponse John was hoping for. He said, "Bob, you know I can't stop you from going, but if you do, there are going to be some serious problems. It's your decision, but you should expect to face some consequences."

What are Bob's options?

57

JUDGE NOT
1 Corinthians 5:1–13; Matthew 7:1–5; Galatians 6:1–5

The girls' discipleship group met weekly to share their lives and pray for one another. Honesty and vulnerability had always been an important element in their fellowship.

It wasn't unusual for the girls to share their struggles and to ask for prayer. What was unusual was Sally's response last week. She shared that she had been hiding something from the group for several months, but had decided that she didn't want to hide her feelings any longer. She had been sleeping with her boyfriend for the last year. They really loved each other, and planned one day to be married. She had prayed about it, and didn't feel it was wrong. In fact, she said, she felt it was more wrong for her to sit in the group week after week and try to feel guilty about a relationship that she thought was wonderful. "I haven't stopped loving Jesus," she continued. "I feel closer to God than I ever have. And I love you guys, too. It's just that I don't agree with you all about this area."

After a moment of silence, Cindy spoke up. "I'm sorry, Sally, but I disagree with you. Your attitude is a breach of our covenant with each other and with God. One of the purposes of this group is to bring our lives under the shaping of God and his Word. I care about you, and I love you, but I feel you should have the integrity to leave the group if you don't share our common vision and goals."

Some of the girls agreed with Cindy. Others came to the support of Sally.

What are the group's options?

58

DISCIPLE OR DOORMAT?
Matthew 18:21–35

This was the fourth time that George had caught Phil lying to him. He knew that Phil was a new Christian, and he was trying to be patient, but George was beginning to feel like a doormat. Every time he confronted Phil, Phil would get humble, apologize, and promise that it wouldn't happen again.

But it does happen again. That's why he was reluctant to trust Phil last Friday morning when he asked to borrow his lab notes. But he knew that he was supposed to forgive and forget, so—against his better judgment—George passed them on.

Well, Phil copied the lab notes almost verbatim. Fortunately the teacher didn't notice, but George was absolutely outraged. He couldn't believe Phil had snaked him again after all the apologies and warnings of the last time.

When Phil came to George to ask for forgiveness, George had had enough. "No, you are not forgiven. You're a liar and a cheat, and I'm through trusting you. I don't care if you flunk out. That's it. Period."

Was George's response right? Should he forgive Phil and be willing to trust him again?

What are George's options?

59

UNHEALTHY FRIENDSHIPS

1 Corinthians 6:14–18; 1 Corinthians 15:33; Matthew 9:10–13

Aaron's parents aren't too pleased with the kids he's been hanging around lately. They're worried about how much influence these other guys are having on Aaron. He can understand their fear, but how is he supposed to have a ministry if he never hangs around anybody but Christians? He accuses his parents of being too judgmental. They accuse Aaron of being naive.

Maybe they're both wrong, or maybe they're both right. But one thing is clear. His parents have laid down the law. They don't want him hanging around that crowd any more.

What are Aaron's options?

60

CHEAT FOR YOUR NEIGHBOR AS FOR YOURSELF
Ephesians 4:15; Galatians 6:1–10

Chris, the kid who sits next to you in English, has just asked you for one of the answers on the test you're both taking. You're not sure what to do.

It's not as if Chris is some kind of stranger. At your invitation, he's been coming to youth group for the last three weeks. He's beginning to show some interest in a relationship with God. And you know that Chris needs this grade. If he doesn't pass this test, he'll flunk English, and may have to stay back next year. Chris has even said that he would rather drop out of school than stay back while everybody goes on to their senior year.

You know that the Bible says to love your neighbor. But you also realize that cheating is dishonest. Yet, it would be pretty cold to withhold one answer from a person who faces some tough options if he doesn't pass the test. Is one little answer more important than a person's life?

Last week, on the way home from Bible study, Chris commented that one of the reasons he is interested in Christ is that he feels like he's finally met some people he could count on in the crunch. He's waiting for your response. The teacher will return to the room any minute. It's crunch time.

What are your options?

END